D1064519

Diseases and Disorders

Arthritis

Arthritis

Titles in the Diseases and Disorders series include:

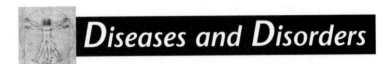

Arthritis

by Barbara Sheen

*Withdrawn
from the
MATC Library*

LIBRARY
MILWAUKEE AREA
TECHNICAL COLLEGE
NORTH CAMPUS
5555 W. Highland Road
Mequon, WI 53092

616.722
S541

No part of this book may be reproduced or used in any form or by any means, electrical, mechanical, or otherwise, including, but not limited to, photocopy, recording, or any information storage and retrieval system, without prior written permission from the publisher.

Library of Congress Cataloging-in-Publication Data

Sheen, Barbara
    Arthritis / by Barbara Sheen.
       p. cm. — (Diseases and disorders series)
    Includes bibliographical references and index.
    Summary: Discusses the types of arthritis, examination and diagnosis, risk factors, treatment and prognosis, and research about the disease.
       ISBN 1-56006-904-X
      1. Arthritis—Juvenile literature. [1. Arthritis. 2. Diseases.]
    I. Title. II. Series.
       RC933 .S4325   2002
       616.7'22—dc21

2001004590

Copyright © 2002 by Lucent Books
an imprint of The Gale Group
10911 Technology Place
San Diego, CA 92127
Printed in the U.S.A.

Table of Contents

"The Most Difficult Puzzles Ever Devised"

CHARLES BEST, ONE of the pioneers in the search for a cure for diabetes, once explained what it is about medical research that intrigued him so. "It's not just the gratification of knowing one is helping people," he confided, "although that probably is a more heroic and selfless motivation. Those feelings may enter in, but truly, what I find best is the feeling of going toe-to-toe with nature, of trying to solve the most difficult puzzles ever devised. The answers are there somewhere, those keys that will solve the puzzle and make the patient well. But how will those keys be found?"

Since the dawn of civilization, nothing has so puzzled people—and often frightened them, as well—as the onset of illness in a body or mind that had seemed healthy before. A seizure, the inability of a heart to pump, the sudden deterioration of muscle tone in a small child—being unable to reverse such conditions or even to understand why they occur was unspeakably frustrating to healers. Even before there were names for such conditions, even before they were understood at all, each was a reminder of how complex the human body was, and how vulnerable.

While our grappling with understanding diseases has been frustrating at times, it has also provided some of humankind's most heroic accomplishments. Alexander Fleming's accidental discovery in 1928 of a mold that could be turned into penicillin has resulted in the saving of untold millions of lives. The isolation of the enzyme insulin has reversed what was once a death sentence for anyone with diabetes. There have been great strides in combating conditions for which there is not yet a cure, too. Medicines can help AIDS patients live longer, diagnostic tools such as mammography and ultrasounds can help doctors find tumors while they are treatable, and laser surgery techniques have made the most intricate, minute operations routine.

This "toe-to-toe" competition with diseases and disorders is even more remarkable when seen in a historical continuum. An astonishing amount of progress has been made in a very short time. Just two hundred years ago, the existence of germs as a cause of some diseases was unknown. In fact, it was less than 150 years ago that a British surgeon named Joseph Lister had difficulty persuading his fellow doctors that washing their hands before delivering a baby might increase the chances of a healthy delivery (especially if they had just attended to a diseased patient)!

Each book in Lucent's *Diseases and Disorders* series explores a disease or disorder and the knowledge that has been accumulated (or discarded) by doctors through the years. Each book also examines the tools used for pinpointing a diagnosis, as well as the various means that are used to treat or cure a disease. Finally, new ideas are presented—techniques or medicines that may be on the horizon.

Frustration and disappointment are still part of medicine, for not every disease or condition can be cured or prevented. But the limitations of knowledge are being pushed outward constantly; the "most difficult puzzles ever devised" are finding challengers every day.

A Disease That Affects Individuals and Society

TARA HAD ALWAYS been a healthy eight-year-old until she woke up one morning with a hot, swollen, and painful knee. She thought she must have sprained it playing basketball. But over the next few weeks the pain intensified, and her other knee, her wrists, and both her feet became hot and swollen as well. The pain was so severe that at times Tara couldn't get out of bed without help. She kept waiting for the pain to go away, but it continued to worsen. Even the smallest movement became difficult. Tara knew that something was seriously wrong. Not long after, Tara was diagnosed with arthritis, a serious disease that afflicts more than 60 million Americans.

Arthritis can strike any of the 150 joints, or places where two bones meet, throughout the human body, hindering the joints from functioning normally. This causes pain and limits the body's ability to bend, flex, twist, turn, and reach. Although rarely fatal, arthritis is an incurable illness. In its mildest forms, it causes only minor pain and harm. However, in its most aggressive forms, it can be extremely painful, causing permanent and serious damage to the joints and changing the lives of its victims forever. Tara, who is now eighteen, describes some of the ways this disease has affected her: "In the last ten years, I've had surgery on both my knees and have taken so many different medicines that I can't even count them. My hands and feet are deformed, and I have to wear special inserts in my shoes. Some days I feel great, and some days I feel like I've been hit by a train. That's just the way it is with arthritis."[1]

Because arthritis is one of the most widespread disabling diseases in the world, it not only causes problems for the afflicted individuals but also has a tremendous impact on society. Arthritis is currently the greatest cause of persistent pain and disability in the United States. It impairs more Americans than heart attacks and strokes combined. Arthritis limits the daily activities of approximately 7 million Americans, and within ten years of their diagnosis, more than 50 percent of these people will be unable to work. Experts estimate that arthritis costs society about $65 billion per year in medical costs, disability payments, and lost income, an amount that exceeds the yearly national income of many emerging nations.

Compounding this problem is the fact that people are living longer. Since arthritis often strikes the elderly, scientists predict that about 20 million more Americans, about one in every five, will contract arthritis within the next ten years. Of these, more than 10 million will become disabled. Consequently, arthritis's impact on

A pair of swollen hands shows the disabling effects of rheumatoid arthritis.

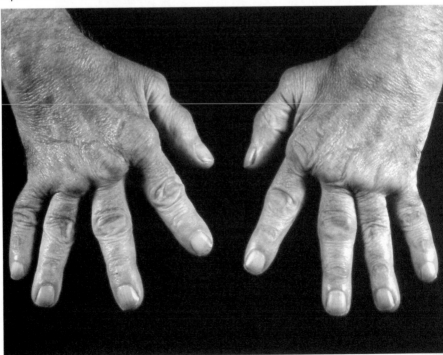

individuals and society is expected to balloon. It is estimated that by 2010 almost every American will have a friend or family member with arthritis.

Because arthritis's impact is so far-reaching, it is important that people understand more about it. By learning more about what causes arthritis, how to best treat it, and the challenges it presents, friends and family members will gain a better understanding of how to provide arthritis sufferers with appropriate support and help. Patients and their families will be able to make better choices about their treatment and learn better ways to manage and control the disease. This type of knowledge should help limit the disabling progress of the disease, lessening its damaging effects on individuals and its cost to society. At eighteen, Tara has learned quite a bit about arthritis and how to manage it. She is a busy and popular high school senior. Like many other teenagers, she goes to school, has an active social life, and looks forward to adulthood. She explains, "I want to go to college and study to be a kindergarten teacher, and I want to get married and have a bunch of kids. Lots of things are harder for me because of my arthritis. But most of the time, my arthritis doesn't slow me down. Except for taking medicine, I live pretty much like everyone else."[2]

Chapter 1

What Is Arthritis?

ARTHRITIS IS A skeletal disease characterized by swelling, inflammation, stiffness, limited movement, and pain. Unlike normal minor aches and pains that everyone occasionally feels, arthritis pain is long-lasting. It does not go away within a few days like the temporary pain caused by injuries or vigorous exercise. Instead, it is persistent, long-term, and, in many cases, quite severe. Even in cases when the pain is less severe, it is still a constant dull ache.

Dr. Thomas Sydenham, a fifteenth-century physician who was one of the earliest physicians to treat and study arthritis, described the pain experienced by one of his patients:

> The victim goes to bed. About two in the morning he is awakened by severe pain. The pain is like that of a dislocation, and yet the parts feel as if cold water were poured over them. Now it is a violent stretching and tearing of ligaments. Now it is a gnawing pain, and now a pressure and tightening. The part affected can not bear the weight of the bedclothes, nor the jar of a person walking in the room. The night is spent in torture.[3]

Two Different Groups of Arthritis

The severity of the pain depends on the type of arthritis a person has. Though there are more than one hundred different varieties of arthritis, all of them fit into two categories: degenerative arthritis and inflammatory arthritis. There are a number of differences between degenerative and inflammatory arthritis. But, despite their differences, both groups cause the joints and cartilage that surrounds the joints to deteriorate, resulting in pain and limited joint movement.

Bone Grinding Against Bone

Of the two categories of arthritis, degenerative arthritis is the most common form of arthritis. It affects more than 21 million people in the United States today. Most types of degenerative arthritis usually take many years to develop. They result when injury, overuse, repetitive motion, or aging gradually break down the cartilage.

Cartilage is a tough, rubbery tissue that protects and cushions the joints. It is made of a protein called collagen, and is quite smooth. Cartilage acts as a natural shock absorber providing a slick surface

Pictured is the left knee of a man who is suffering from a severe case of osteoarthritis.

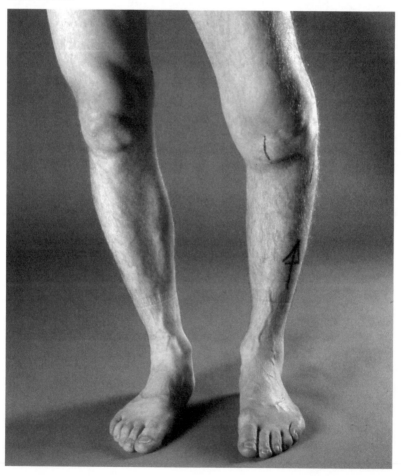

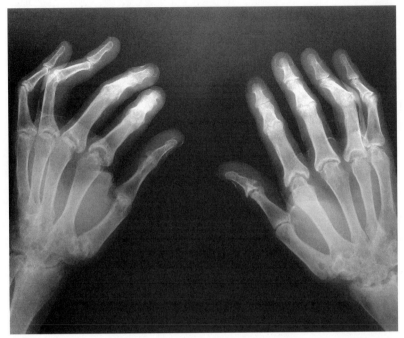

An X ray reveals the degeneration of cartilage in the fingers of an arthritis sufferer.

for the bone ends to glide across. This keeps them from rubbing against each other and wearing away. In fact, according to arthritis expert, Dr. Barry Fox, "There is not a single man-made substance that's more resilient, a better shock absorber, or lower in friction than cartilage."[4]

Just as cartilage protects the joint, cartilage is, in turn, protected by a fluid, known as synovial fluid, that is produced deep inside the joint lining. Synovial fluid is released onto the cartilage whenever the joint is moved. It acts like oil, keeping the cartilage slippery so that the joint can move smoothly across it. However, as a result of injury, overuse, or aging, the production of synovial fluid gradually decreases and finally stops completely. Without this fluid acting as a lubricant, the cartilage slowly becomes thinner and thinner, eventually wearing away entirely. This leaves the joint exposed and unprotected. When this happens, the resulting grinding of bone against bone causes the joint to erode and lose its natural shape. In an attempt to protect the joint from this destruction, extra bone forms at the ends.

But since the ends of the new bone are unprotected by cartilage and synovial fluid, they quickly become deformed, changing from smooth to bumpy. As a result, the joint becomes difficult to move. At the same time, as a result of the damage to the cartilage and bone, mild inflammation causes the joint to swell and produces more pain. The end result of this process is the development of degenerative arthritis. Osteoarthritis and carpal tunnel syndrome are both varieties of degenerative arthritis. Osteoarthritis, in fact, is the single-most widespread variety of arthritis. It currently afflicts one in every ten people in the United States. It generally affects large weight-bearing joints such as the lower back, hips, knees, and ankles on only one side of the body. Experts consider it to be a serious but manageable condition typified by pain that increases as the joint is used and stiffness that occurs when the joint is at rest.

Out-of-Control Inflammation

Inflammation plays a key role in the second category of arthritis known as inflammatory arthritis, which often develops suddenly and progresses rapidly. It affects many small joints such as the fingers, knuckles, wrists, elbows, shoulders, knees, and ankles. Because of how quickly it progresses, inflammatory arthritis can be extremely destructive. As a result, inflammatory arthritis is usually more serious than degenerative arthritis. It can be very painful, and because of the stress it puts on the body, it may lead to the development of other diseases such as anemia, heart disease, and a variety of eye disorders.

Inflammatory arthritis usually occurs when the immune system, which protects the body from infection and disease, malfunctions. For reasons that are not yet understood, in inflammatory arthritis, rather than attacking and destroying bacteria and other unwelcome invaders, the immune system goes haywire and attacks healthy cells that protect and line the joints.

Normally, when germs that cause infection invade the body, blood rushes to the infected area, and white blood cells seek out and destroy the germs. Pus and other powerful agents are also produced to combat the infection. As a result of the rush of blood, pus, and chemicals, the infected area becomes hot, red, and swollen. Heat, redness, and swelling are characteristic of inflammation, which normally disappears when an infection has healed.

In inflammatory arthritis, however, white blood cells mistake healthy cells in the joint lining for germs and attack them. Pus and other destructive chemicals also rush to the joint, causing the joint to become inflamed, painful, and swollen. In order to combat the attacking white blood cells, cells within the joint grow. In the joint's rush to produce enough of these counterattacking cells to protect itself, the new cells divide abnormally and mutate. The immune system then releases powerful chemicals to destroy these mutant cells.

An electron micrograph shows stages of damage on the surface of a thighbone.

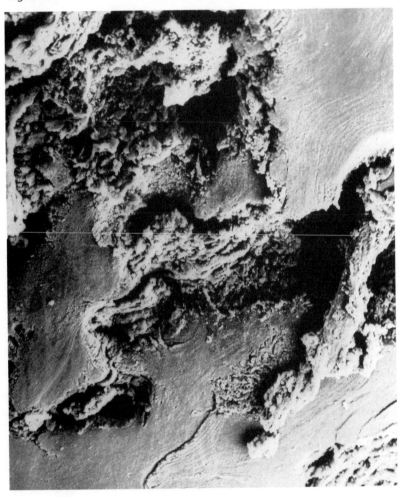

The chemicals eat away not only at the mutant cells but also at the bone and cartilage. The damage from these chemicals causes more blood to rush to the area, worsening the inflammation and further injuring the cartilage and bone. Trying to protect the joint, more mutant cells are produced, causing more chemicals to be released, and the inflammatory process is repeated again and again, resulting in more and more damage.

Inflammation is normally beneficial. It plays a key role in helping the immune system by increasing the flow of blood that carries infection-fighting white blood cells and chemicals to the infected area. However, in inflammatory arthritis, when there is no actual infection threatening the body, the inflammatory process becomes the enemy, causing destruction rather than recovery. Scientists call this process an autoimmune response, and diseases such as inflammatory arthritis are known as autoimmune diseases.

Although experts do not know what causes autoimmune diseases, some hypothesize that an unknown virus triggers a change in the joint cells, causing the white blood cells to attack. Others believe that certain people have a genetic tendency to develop autoimmune diseases. No matter what the reason, when the inflammatory process is not controlled as it normally is by the body, or by medication, the joint becomes deformed. As a result of inflammatory arthritis, there is pain and loss of mobility, and permanent disability often occurs.

Types of Inflammatory Arthritis

There are many types of inflammatory arthritis. The most common types include ankylosing spondylitis, in which the bones of the spine become inflamed and fuse together; gout, which affects the big toe; juvenile arthritis, which attacks children under the age of sixteen; lupus, which affects not only the bones but the kidneys, heart, skin, and brain; and rheumatoid arthritis, which affects 2.1 million Americans, making it second, only to osteoarthritis, in the number of people it afflicts.

Rheumatoid arthritis is the most painful and disabling form of arthritis. It often spreads rapidly throughout the body, resulting in severe inflammation that frequently causes fever and damages multiple joints. It usually affects the smaller joints on both sides of the

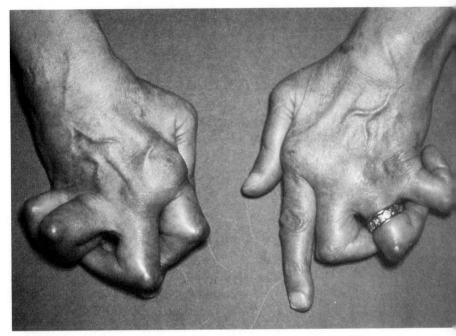

Rheumatoid arthritis can disintegrate bones and lead to permanent joint deformity.

body, such as those in the wrists, elbows, and ankles. In some cases it can affect almost every joint in the body. A patient with this problem tells about her experience: "My knees are what started it. Then it went to my ankles, wrist, and elbows. Then it entered my neck and affected everything around it like my shoulders, back, and jaw."[5]

Rheumatoid arthritis generally affects at least five joints. It causes cartilage to tear and bones to disintegrate, resulting in severe pain, permanent joint deformity, and restricted mobility. Because the inflammation in rheumatoid arthritis is so severe and the joint destruction occurs so rapidly, patients with rheumatoid arthritis are more likely to be confined to a wheelchair than are patients with any other type of arthritis.

Repetitive Movement

Although there is no way to prevent the development of arthritis, experts believe that there are certain environmental and lifestyle factors that put people at greater risk by weakening the joints and making them more susceptible to arthritis. Among these factors are repetitive movements like those performed in certain jobs, joint injury, stress caused by heavy lifting, and some athletic activities.

The idea that repetitive movement, injury, and prolonged stress could result in arthritis was first investigated by an Austrian scientist, Hans Selye, in 1935. As part of an experiment, Selye repeatedly injected a foreign substance into the joints of laboratory animals. He then observed how their bodies adapted to this repeated stress in a number of ways. Selye theorized that, although these adaptations served to protect the animals over the short term, if the animal were repeatedly exposed to stress, infection, or injury, this protective response would actually damage the joint. Selye was proven correct. Arthritis is often caused, or intensified, by repeated injury or stress to a joint.

People who perform certain jobs are at a greater risk of developing arthritis than those in other professions are. For example, construction workers and coal miners repeatedly bend and lift heavy things, putting constant stress on their joints. Assembly line workers, tailors, musicians, and hairstylists, who perform constant repet-

People who perform repetitive activities, such as styling hair, are at risk of developing arthritis.

itive activities, also have an increased risk. Arthritis expert Dr. Earl J. Brewer Jr. describes one such person:

> Holding a comb tightly in her left hand as she expertly manipulated my hair, clipping and snipping the ends, she suddenly winced and lowered her arm. She bent her left thumb and rubbed it gingerly. I saw that the base of her thumb was enlarged and knew she was in pain. I asked her what had happened to her thumb. Twenty-five years of barbering, she replied, bending her thumb to show its squared off look.[6]

It has been estimated that problems caused by repetitive stress affect more than 185,000 workers in the United States each year. As a result, many develop arthritis.

Weight Stress

A second kind of stress to the joints comes from persistent stress caused by athletic activities. Runners, gymnasts, and other athletes who perform high-impact sports that persistently stress the joints are also at risk. Running exerts a force of ten times a person's body weight on the hips and knees. This force puts tremendous stress on the cartilage and synovial fluid, which must work extra hard to protect the joints. However, when this stress becomes persistent, as it does when a person runs frequently, the synovial fluid will eventually dry up and the cartilage will wear away. This occurred in one former runner, who recalls his experience: "I was in the Army for twenty years, and ran like a deer. I had little problem with my joints. Then one morning I woke up and my right knee was swollen like a balloon with immense pain. I went to the doctor and submitted to various tests. I now have been told that I have arthritis in my right knee."[7]

Similarly, ballet dancers who go from flat foot to the pointe position thousands of times in their dancing careers put incredible stress on their toes, ankles, knees, and hips. Over time, this type of stress traumatizes the joints, resulting in chronic injuries and the development of arthritis. One ballerina's experience exemplifies this:

Ballet movements such as going from flat foot to the pointe position puts great stress on the lower body.

She began feeling pain in her right hip that didn't respond to all the usual treatments of Ben-Gay, hot baths, and good warm-ups. At first she thought it might be a pulled or strained muscle from overdoing a swiveling step, and that it would heal on its own accord. Through the early fall of that year, on tour with the New York City Ballet, her hip continued to ache, but she kept dancing. By October, after it had been getting steadily worse for three months, she sought a professional opinion: "This was the first of many doctors I would visit over the next few years," she writes, "all of whom, after taking x-rays, gave me the same diagnosis, the very last one I wanted to hear." She had arthritis, a word, she writes, that "for a dancer is the equivalent of a death sentence. . . . I associated arthritis with old age, but I was only thirty-eight and at the height of my physical abilities as a dancer in every way, except for my right hip." That hip, the x-rays showed, had the cartilage erosion of someone twice her age.[8]

Previous Injuries

Past injury to a joint can also be a risk factor. Not only do past injuries often cause permanent damage to cartilage, but they stress uninjured joints that are overused to compensate for the injured joint. For example, if a knee is injured, the victim may limp. This puts unusual stress on the uninjured knee, which may result in arthritis in the future.

Experts agree that an injury to a joint increases the chances of developing arthritis in that joint. Impact injuries, which are common in sports such as football, basketball, and hockey, often result in many professional and amateur athletes developing arthritis. In fact, studies have shown that almost half of all professional football players contract arthritis, with one out of every three requiring corrective surgery. This is also quite common in former high school and college athletes. Arthritis expert Dr. Joel Rutstein tells about a patient whose past injury to his knee led to arthritis: "A fifty-eight-year-old man is seen in consultation because of severe right knee pain. When he was in college, he sustained an injury to the cartilage of the right knee while playing football. In his forties he started having pain over the right knee once again. This patient has degenerative arthritis of the knee, which has occurred some thirty years later. This is a fairly typical event."[9]

Being Overweight

Another factor that increases the risk of arthritis is being overweight. Extra weight puts extra strain on the hips and the knees, since with each step the stress on these joints is equal to three to ten times a person's body weight. According to Dr. Barry Fox, "That extra ten pounds around the middle may translate to an extra one hundred pounds slamming away on certain joints at certain times."[10] For example, when a one-hundred-pound person climbs a flight of stairs, three to ten times that person's weight presses on his or her knees due to gravity. So, at a minimum there are 300 pounds of pressure on those knees. If the person gains thirty pounds, the amount of pressure on the knees will increase to a minimum of 390 pounds. This type of extra stress affects the cartilage, synovial fluid, and joints the same way that persistent stress does.

Studies confirm a link between the development of arthritis and being overweight. Almost 50 percent of the people in the United States who develop degenerative arthritis in the knee have been overweight for at least three years. In addition, studies sponsored by the Arthritis Foundation confirm that overweight people who lose at least eleven pounds over a ten-year period cut their risk of developing arthritis in half.

A Widespread Disease

Although some of these risk factors may be avoided, there are no guarantees in preventing a person from getting arthritis. One hundred million people worldwide currently suffer from arthritis, including one out of every six people in America. One million new patients develop arthritis each year.

Juvenile Arthritis

Often thought to be a disease of the elderly, arthritis actually affects people of all ages. A sufferer who was diagnosed with arthritis as a teenager recalls her own surprise: "Everyone in my family was shocked when the doc said I had arthritis. We all thought that only old people got arthritis, not kids. My granny had it. I wasn't supposed to have it. I was only fourteen. I thought the doc had to be wrong, so did the rest of my family. But the doc wasn't wrong, we were. Boy, did we have a lot to learn. Anyone can get arthritis, grannies and babies too. It's not an old person's disease."[11]

Approximately 285,000 children, or about one in every 1,000 children in the United States, are afflicted with juvenile arthritis, the most serious crippling disease of childhood. Many of these children

This three-year-old child suffers from juvenile chronic arthritis, a highly crippling disease among the young.

exhibit their first symptoms, which often include pain and swelling in four or more joints, a high fever, and a rash caused by inflammation, by three years old. Experts do not know why juvenile arthritis rarely occurs before this age. But they agree that once it does occur, it is rarely outgrown. Juvenile arthritis, with its accompanying pain and damaged joints, often afflicts patients for the rest of their lives.

Higher Odds

In addition, females are twice as likely as males to have arthritis. Despite extensive research, experts are unsure why arthritis afflicts so many females. Some theorize that there may be a connection between the production of certain female hormones and arthritis, but there is no conclusive evidence. Currently, 26 million American females suffer from the disease, with a particularly large number suffering from inflammatory arthritis. In fact, 70 percent of rheumatoid arthritis sufferers in the United States are women, and 86 percent of juvenile arthritis sufferers are girls.

African Americans are another group that is hit hard by arthritis. Arthritis is the third most common disease to strike this group. Four million African Americans suffer from some form of arthritis and African American females have a higher rate of arthritis than females in any other ethnic group. In fact, African American females are three times more likely to suffer from lupus than any other group. One in every 250 African American females contracts lupus. Scientists do not know why African American females are so frequently afflicted by the disease, but they suspect that a tendency to develop lupus may be genetically inherited.

Chronic Pain and Limited Mobility

No matter who arthritis strikes, experts agree that it not only physically stresses sufferers but also weakens their emotional state, causing persistent fatigue and accompanying irritability. One sufferer recalls his experience: "I woke up every morning with a sharp burning pain that only got worse as the day went on. By the late afternoon I was tired and miserable. Between the pain and exhaustion, I was worn down and short tempered. All I could think about was going home and putting my feet up, so I could get the weight off my knees."[12]

In the face of this lingering pain, many people become inactive. This lack of movement weakens the muscles that surround the joints, which result in even weaker and more painful joints. According to the Arthritis Foundation, "When you don't move a joint regularly, the muscles around it weaken and become tight. The joint also stiffens because it is not moved regularly. When you try to move, the joint and muscles hurt from arthritis pain and from not being moved regularly."[13]

Compounding this problem is the fact that the destruction of bone that causes the joints to deform can also cause the tendons around the joints to slip out of place and harden. This can result in the joint freezing into a partially contracted position that makes full use of the joint impossible, and may lead to permanent disability.

Another serious concern is the possibility of the autoimmune reaction, with its accompanying inflammation, spreading to organs near the afflicted joints. This most often occurs in severe inflammatory arthritis when inflammation enters the bloodstream from the joints and travels to the membranes surrounding other nearby organs such as the heart, lungs, and eyes, which then become inflamed. This can cause difficulty breathing, chest pains, abnormal heartbeat, blocked blood vessels, nerve damage, and dry tear ducts.

Rheumatoid nodules, like the one on this elbow, form in response to physical stress on a joint.

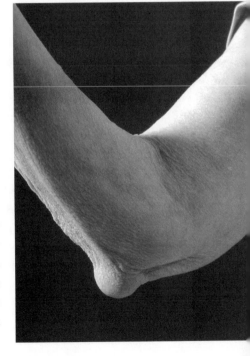

How serious the consequences of arthritis may be depends on how quickly the disease progresses. This varies from individual to individual. Arthritis is very unpredictable. It may be quite severe in some patients, affecting a large number of joints and progressing rapidly, or it may be mild, affecting only a few joints with slow progress. In cases when the disease progresses quickly, the damage to the joints is most devastating. A patient's father recalls, "Within three months my daughter had some forty-six joints inflamed or swollen. At times she could not get out of bed. At times she could not stand for us to touch her."[14]

Flare-Ups and Remission

Even the most severe cases of arthritis often progress with stops and starts. Periods of intense pain combined with increased stiffness and swelling, known as flare-ups, are mixed with near normal periods, known as remission. Periods of flare-ups and remission can last for days, weeks, months, or years.

Pain during flare-ups can be intolerable. During this time, even the simplest of movements can be unbearable. A juvenile arthritis sufferer discusses how flare-ups affect her:

> Flare-ups are the worst. The pain is unbelievable. I just want to roll up into a little ball and disappear. Of course, I can't roll up. I can't even get out of bed because it hurts too much to move. Forget about trying to get dressed or going to school. I feel so crummy that I don't even want to talk on the phone! All I can do is lay in bed like a stick and rest until my medicine kicks in and I start feeling human again. [15]

Experts believe that during periods of flare-up, especially early in the disease, sufferers experience the most damage to their joints. During these periods, inflammation is at its worst, resulting in extremely rapid bone and cartilage destruction and the deforming and dislocation of bones. The damage or disability that occurs during flare-ups is permanent. Because of this, during periods of remission, people with arthritis feel better but still experience some pain and stiffness due to the existing damage to their joints.

In general, remission usually occurs as a result of treatment. However, it can also take place spontaneously and can last for years before another flare-up occurs. Experts do not understand why this happens. Studies have shown that patients who do not have a particular chemical, known as the rheumatoid factor, in their blood, are more likely to have milder cases of arthritis and longer periods of remission than patients who have this chemical in their blood. The reason why this occurs still remains a mystery to scientists. What is not a mystery, however, is how far-reaching arthritis is and how much damage it causes.

Chapter 2

Diagnosis and Treatment

A RTHRITIS IS AN incurable disease that can be successfully managed when diagnosis is made early. Arthritis is not difficult to diagnose. When patients complain of persistent, unexplained pain and stiffness in their joints, doctors usually suspect arthritis. However, the diagnostic picture is complicated by the problem of distinguishing between the different forms of arthritis. Determining which of the more than one hundred types of arthritis a patient may have can be tricky because many types share the same symptoms. With this in mind, doctors may have to perform a large number of different blood tests over a prolonged period of time in order to pinpoint the exact variety. Many patients report that, although their doctors were sure that they were suffering from some form of arthritis, it took weeks, and in some cases months, to conclusively establish which form of arthritis afflicted them.

Initially, doctors look for general symptoms commonly found in all types of arthritis. These include recurring or constant pain in the joints, joint stiffness, difficulty moving, and inflammation. If these symptoms are present, the doctor will study the severity of inflammation and the joints involved to determine whether the patient is suffering from degenerative or inflammatory arthritis. Once this is resolved, specific symptoms are examined in order to ascertain which specific type of arthritis the patient is afflicted with.

Specific Symptoms Define Specific Forms of Arthritis

Because different forms of arthritis affect different joints, identifying which joints are involved helps to distinguish among the various

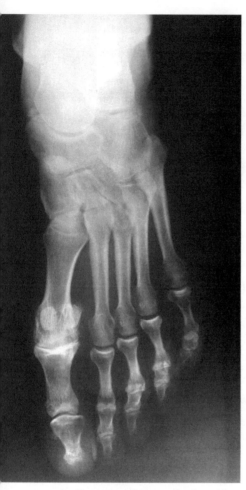

An X ray reveals the early signs of gout in a big toe.

types of arthritis. For example, in some cases, such as gout, in which the only joint that is usually affected is the large joint of the big toe, which becomes painful and inflamed, diagnosis is simplified. Identifying ankylosing spondylitis, a form of arthritis that attacks the joints in the spine, is also relatively simple.

Some forms are harder to identify because they affect multiple joints and share other symptoms such as fatigue, lack of appetite, fever, and numbness in the hands and feet. This makes it hard for the doctor to determine exactly what form of arthritis the patient is suffering from and further complicates the diagnosis. A patient whose symptoms were common to both rheumatoid arthritis and lupus recalls the problem her doctor had determining which of these disorders she suffered from: "I was in agony. First my knees swelled, and were hot and painful. My neck and back were next. It quickly spread to my hands and feet, which alternated between aching terribly and feeling completely numb. The pain was excruciating. At first my doctor wasn't sure how to treat me. He believed the problem was rheumatoid arthritis, but confessed that it might also have been lupus."[16]

X Rays and Blood Tests

To overcome these complications and accurately match patients' symptoms to individual types of arthritis, doctors may administer X rays and blood tests. X rays allow doctors to see inside the joints to determine whether joint and cartilage damage exists and, if it does, the type and extent of the damage. This is particularly helpful in distinguishing between rheumatoid arthritis and osteoarthritis, because the appearance of the damaged joints and surrounding tissue differs. For example, X rays of patients with rheumatoid arthritis show swelling of the joints and surrounding tissue, while X rays of patients with osteoarthritis show worn-down, uneven joints with small deformed bony growths on the ends.

X rays, which are often taken of multiple joints, also help doctors by providing a baseline view of the patient's joints. This provides a reference for evaluating and comparing the current and future extent of bone and cartilage damage. In addition, X rays are used to rule out the possibility of bone cancer, a disease that has symptoms similar to those of arthritis, such as fatigue and persistent unexplained joint pain.

Despite the evidence that X rays provide, some cases also require the use of blood tests. Substances found in the blood verify the presence of inflammation, infection, and injury, and provide further evidence of specific forms of arthritis. By examining the number of red

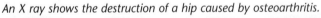

An X ray shows the destruction of a hip caused by osteoarthritis.

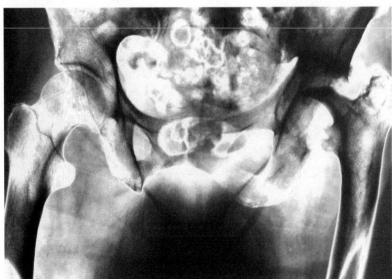

and white blood cells, a blood test can determine the presence and extent of inflammation. A low red-blood-cell count verifies that inflammation is present. Moreover, during inflammation, blood cells clump together and become heavier than normal. Tests that measure how fast blood cells fall to the bottom of a test tube are a good indicator of the level of inflammation. Since the heaviest cells fall the fastest, the quicker the rate the cells fall, the higher the level of inflammation. High levels of inflammation confirm that the patient is afflicted with inflammatory arthritis, while low levels indicate that the patient is a victim of degenerative arthritis.

In addition, abnormal amounts of certain chemicals in the blood signal the presence of gout or lupus. Blood tests also analyze the level of antibodies, or proteins, found in the blood. The presence of the rheumatoid factor, for example, a specific antibody that is found in two-thirds of the people who have rheumatoid arthritis, is a strong indicator that the patient is suffering from rheumatoid arthritis. And when high levels of the rheumatoid factor are found, the need for aggressive treatment is evident.

Individualized Treatment

Experts agree that treating arthritis early is the most effective way to reduce the risk of permanent disability. Because there are so many types of arthritis, and symptoms, the number of joints involved, and severity vary greatly, treatment is tailored to meet the needs of individual patients. No matter what form of arthritis a patient is afflicted with, treatment focuses on relieving pain and inflammation, improving joint function, and reducing further joint damage to help the patient live a normal life. According to the Arthritis Research Campaign, "All forms of arthritis can be relieved to some extent by treatment even if they can't be cured." [17]

Medication is generally prescribed as the primary form of treatment for arthritis. Many patients are also advised to combine medication and exercise to combat their symptoms. Experts believe that the combination of medicine, which relieves pain and inflammation and slows the progress of the disease, and exercise, which maintains the flexibility and mobility of the joints, is the best way to help arthritis patients. By reducing arthritis sufferers' pain and helping them to

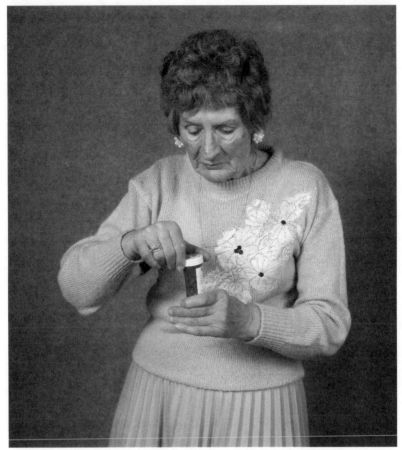

A woman with arthritis struggles to open a bottle of pain medication.

regain their mobility, this combination allows people with arthritis to lead more productive lives.

Three Types of Drugs

There are three distinct types of medication that are used to treat arthritis. The first type, nonsteroidal anti-inflammatory drugs, or NSAIDs, are used to reduce pain, stiffness, and inflammation, resulting in improved mobility. Widely used since their discovery in 1897, they come in nonprescription forms such as aspirin and ibuprofen, and in a large variety of more powerful prescription forms. NSAIDs work by blocking chemicals in the body that cause pain and inflammation. Since arthritis is incurable, once people are afflicted with it, they will continue to suffer from it for the rest of their lives. Consequently, most arthritis sufferers who take medicine such as NSAIDs to relieve pain take this medicine for many years. Kathy Cochran Angel, an arthritis patient and expert who has taken NSAIDs most of her life, explains, "Since my early twenties I have taken ibuprofen every day. If I don't take this medicine for three consecutive days, my joints become stiff and painful."[18]

The second type of drugs used to treat arthritis are steroids. Steroids are extremely powerful, man-made copies of inflammation-fighting hormones found in the human body. Generally used to relieve severe symptoms, steroids stop inflammation entirely by suppressing the immune system. As a result, once the inflammation is eliminated, the pain caused by the inflammation also ceases. This immediate relief from pain and inflammation allows patients taking steroids to almost miraculously regain their freedom of movement. Doctors report that within days of being treated with steroids, arthritis patients who could barely walk because of pain and inflammation have been able to run.

The third type of drugs, disease-modifying antirheumatic drugs, or DMARDs, fight autoimmune reactions. Consequently, they are used mainly to treat inflammatory arthritis. DMARDs include some of the newest drugs used to treat arthritis today. Like the other two types, DMARDs relieve inflammation, stiffness, and pain. In addition, they also slow the progress of arthritis by modifying the way the immune system works, providing patients with long-term joint mobility. According to Dr. Barry Fox, "Disease modifying antirheumatic drugs attempt to reduce the symptoms of arthritis and the accompanying tissue damage by slowing the growth and reproduction of white blood cells. By interfering with white blood cells, which are involved in the inflammation process, joint pain and swelling is relieved, slowing the progression of tissue damage."[19]

Many patients agree that treatment with DMARDs helps them manage their arthritis more successfully. It not only relieves their pain but also allows them to regain mobility that they thought they had lost permanently. A user of DMARDs who experienced these results explains: "It's marvelous. Since I started taking it, I can't believe how well I feel. I'm a new woman. It has changed my life for the better. I'm doing the sort of things that I thought I'd never be able to do again, like playing golf and taking brisk long walks. I thought I had to give those things up forever." [20]

Side Effects and Health Risks of Drugs

Although treatment with medicine can be successful, as with any drugs, there are health risks and side effects. Among the most serious side effects are ulcers accompanied by bleeding within the stomach and intestines. In fact, the number of people experiencing this problem is so great that many patients must take additional medicine to prevent stomach ulcers. And 5 percent of arthritis patients must discontinue certain drug treatment because of this side effect. An arthritis patient who suffered from bleeding ulcers describes the problems with medication she encountered:

> I was taking lots of aspirin each day. The doctor switched me to a prescription medicine. He thought it would be safer and more effective. Everything seemed to be going along fine, until, suddenly, it hit me. I developed bleeding ulcers without any warning, and had to be rushed to the hospital. Being a curious person, when I came home from the hospital I started researching the medicine I'd taken. I found out that it could cause stomach ulcers and internal bleeding without warning. That is exactly what happened to me. I also found out that it could cause death. I was lucky. I could have died. [21]

Other patients complain of nausea, mouth ulcers, hair loss, skin rash, fatigue, blurred vision, and memory loss caused by medicines used to treat arthritis. "I looked, and felt like a zombie," one patient reports. "I was tired 24-7. My hair started getting thin, and every time I brushed my teeth, I spit blood. My fingernails kept breaking off too. The doc said it was perfectly normal. . . . It was not normal, it was scary. I could have been the star of a horror movie. When my hair started falling out, I called it quits. I'd rather be cracky, and swollen, and achy. That drug was not for me." [22]

Arthritis treatments that alter the immune system can present even more troubling side effects and serious health risks. Because these drugs suppress the immune system and mask symptoms of arthritis and other diseases, users are unaware that they may be seriously ill and often suffer from undetected infections. Ironically, while these drugs make the user's bones and joints feel better, they also often cause a loss of calcium in the bones, which further weakens already damaged joints and leads to other bone diseases such as osteoporosis, a disease in which the bones become brittle and break easily. Further complicating matters, some arthritis medicines, such as steroids, must be taken in larger and larger doses in order to remain effective because the patients develop a tolerance. As a result, patients cannot simply stop treatment without risking very severe flare-ups. Instead, use of these medicines must be lowered gradually. Consequently, because of their strength and the danger they pose to the user, these drugs are generally used to treat only the sickest patients. According to Dr. Earl J. Brewer, because of these problems, "Most physicians try to use cortisone [a steroid drug] as a last resort or in severe situations, since it is clearly the most effective anti-inflammatory medicine but the side effects make us think carefully before using it."[23]

How Exercise Helps

Major concerns about the side effects that often accompany arthritis medication have led doctors to prescribe exercise as a complementary form of treatment. Research has shown that exercise reduces pain. Exercise causes the body to release endorphins, natural chemicals that give the exerciser a feeling of wellness that reduces stress and eliminates or reduces pain. One arthritis sufferer describes her experience with exercise: "Yes it hurts to move. But if you do it consistently and regularly, then at some point, whether you're just walking or doing aerobic exercise, the endorphins in your brain kick in. That's your natural pain reliever."[24]

Exercise also benefits arthritis patients by improving their mobility, keeping their joints from stiffening, their muscles strong, and their cartilage healthy. In addition, exercise improves balance, flexibility, and overall fitness. By reducing pain and improving mobility, exercise makes people with arthritis feel better. As a result, patients are often able to eliminate or take smaller doses of medicine.

Joint-friendly exercises like yoga can aid in bending and stretching without pain.

Experts agree that a combination of strength-training exercise, flexibility-building exercise, and aerobic exercise is the best regimen for arthritis patients. Strength training, such as training with weights, improves endurance and builds muscle that can better support the joints and protect them from further damage. Similarly, flexibility exercises, such as yoga, increase the exerciser's ability to bend and stretch without pain. Low-impact aerobic exercises such as swimming, walking, and biking build stamina, reduce pain and stress, and generally improve the ability to move.

Exercising in water is a very popular treatment for arthritis patients. Water acts as a natural resistance while supporting the patient's weight and reducing all stress on the joints. In fact, many communities offer special swimming and water exercise classes for people with arthritis. These classes are led by specially trained instructors who design individual programs aimed at helping arthri-

A group of women participates in a water aerobics class, a popular treatment for arthritis patients.

tis patients improve the quality of their lives. A patient who attends a water exercise program explains: "When I sat all day thinking that I was protecting my hip from use, I was in pain for hours. Then when I started the exercise plan and avoided being sedentary, my hip improved to the point where I am rarely bothered with pain and stiffness."[25]

Experts and patients agree that combining exercise with medication can improve arthritis sufferers' lives in many ways. Many believe that the feeling of increased control and independence that these combined treatments offer is crucial. One patient whose life has been improved with medication and exercise says,

> For a long time, things were really going downhill. I was in bad shape. All I could think about was the pain and what was going to happen to me next. I knew if things didn't take a turn for the better, I could wind up seriously disabled. I was worried. I have a family to support. Now, between the medicine and my daily workout, I feel strong again. I'm back in control of my life. Being in control and being able to take care of my family and myself is more important to me than anything else. The medicine and the workouts did that for me.[26]

When Surgery Is Needed

Unfortunately, even though exercise and medicine help many patients successfully manage their arthritis, this combination does not provide relief for everyone. Because of the unpredictability of arthritis flare-ups and the side effects and health risks of medication, some patients do not respond favorably to treatment with drugs or exercise. Plagued with pain, these patients are often afflicted with extremely severe cases of arthritis in which their joints have become so damaged and deformed that treatment with exercise is impractical. As recently as forty years ago, such patients frequently became seriously disabled or bedridden. Their arthritis forced them to lead extremely restricted lives. But today, joint replacement surgery, in which damaged joints are removed and replaced with artificial parts, provides these patients with another form of treatment that

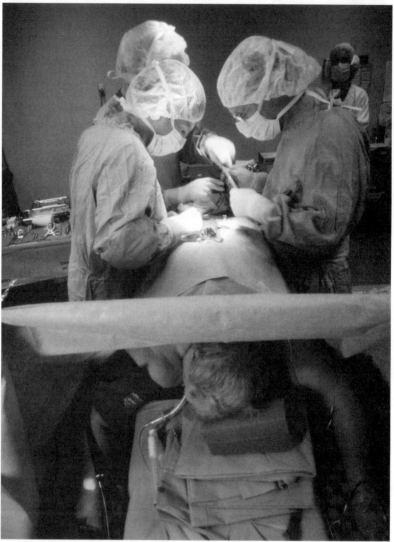

A patient receives neurosurgery to treat the arthritis in his back.

can relieve their pain, correct their joint deformities, and restore their mobility.

It is possible to replace almost every joint in the body with an artificial joint. Damaged shoulders, ankles, and knuckles have all been successfully replaced. However, the most commonly replaced joints are the hip and the knee. Currently, an estimated 150,000 hip joints and an estimated 130,000 knee joints are replaced in the United States each year.

No matter what joint is replaced, joint replacement surgery is technical and complex. Because of this, it is not usually an option unless other forms of treatment have failed. An orthopedic surgeon, a doctor who specializes in surgically treating diseases of the bones, usually performs joint replacement surgery. While the patient is under anesthesia the doctor makes an incision in the damaged joint and detaches the tendons that surround and support the bone. Next, the joint is dislodged, and the diseased and deformed parts of the bone are cut away. The missing parts of the joint are replaced with plastic or metal substitutes that are cemented into place. Like a puzzle piece, the joint is fitted back into its place, and the tendons are carefully reattached. Finally, the wound is closed. The patient generally remains in the hospital for about a week.

Depending on the joint that was replaced, the patient may need to use crutches for at least another six weeks. It often takes another month before the patient fully recuperates, but the severe pain from arthritis is usually relieved immediately. Complications from joint replacement surgery are rare, but, as with any other surgery, there is a risk of infection, and blood clots. In addition, the new joint can sometimes slip out of place, and the cement surrounding it can crack and break into small pieces. Complicating matters, replacement joints have a limited life span of about ten to fifteen years. However, statistics show that 95 percent of the patients who receive joint replacement surgery report excellent long-term results. In fact, these patients report that surgery eliminated or greatly reduced their pain and restored their mobility.

Experts agree that the results of joint replacement surgery can often be sensational, getting bedridden and wheelchair-bound arthritis patients back on their feet. As one patient who had both hips replaced explains,

> Prior to the surgeries, I was constantly aware of my physical limitations. I was in pain and could not do normal tasks easily, or sometimes at all. I observed myself transforming from a strong, athletic person into a seriously impaired individual with no great

hope of returning to the person I had been. All this changed dramatically following my surgeries. I regained mobility and strength, and felt like I had reason to hope. Normal day-to-day tasks that previously had been difficult reverted to normal day-to-day tasks. I could even think of playing tennis again. I am so much better off than I was."[27]

Surgery and exercise treatments can greatly assist arthritis sufferers in getting back to normal day-to-day activities.

Treatment for a Full, Productive Life

Current arthritis treatments offer patients a wide variety of options, including hundreds of different medications, exercise programs, and surgery, all aimed at improving their lives. As one thankful patient attests, "When my grandmother was diagnosed with arthritis a few decades ago, the milder cases were simply put on aspirin, over twenty a day! If they didn't die of a bleeding ulcer, they were quickly disabled from the disease. As much as I hate having arthritis, I'm glad I have it now. Never before have we had so many treatment options. We have so many to choose from. As a result most of us will live full, productive lives."[28]

Chapter 3

Alternative Treatment

ALTHOUGH CONVENTIONAL TREATMENTS for arthritis offer patients several options, many patients and their doctors seek alternative treatment for a variety of reasons. The main reason is the failure of drug treatment. Other reasons patients seek alternatives include side effects that present serious health risks, the desire to find a cure for arthritis, and the desire to relieve the persistent pain that conventional medicine may subdue but not eliminate.

Use of alternative treatments among people with arthritis is so widespread that the Arthritis Foundation estimates that 94 percent of all arthritis patients try alternative treatments, spending a total of $6 million a year. Alternatives range from physical treatments such as acupuncture, chiropractic treatment, and massage to treatments that use the mind to control pain such as tai chi and meditation. Dietary supplements such as herbs and vitamins are also often explored. In fact, dietary supplements are the most popular form of alternative treatment.

Although some forms of alternative treatments have been widely studied, including the use of acupuncture and meditation, others, such as color therapy, have not. Unlike conventional treatments, alternative treatments are not regulated by the U.S. government and have not been conclusively proven to have a specific benefit. Some people avoid alternatives because they are not regulated, but others are willing to learn for themselves.

An arthritis patient who experienced a number of side effects while being treated with traditional medicine and became worried about the medicine's effect on her body explains why she turned to alternative treatment: "A friend of mine recommended I go to an herbalist. She [the herbalist] put me on a combination of herbs and vitamins. She also taught me how to meditate. I feel like I'm headed in the right direction. I feel better. I'm in less pain, and the treatment is natural, so I'm not worried about what it will do to me."[29]

Physical Treatments

Acupuncture is one of the most widely studied alternative treatments for arthritis. In a number of studies sponsored by the National Institutes of Health, acupuncture has been found to help relieve chronic pain. A complete understanding of why acupuncture relieves pain eludes arthritis experts. However, the most commonly accepted theory is that acupuncture causes a biological response that stimulates the body to produce endorphins, the body's natural painkiller. Recommended by the World Health Organization and

An acupuncturist applies needles to the knees and hands of a rheumatoid arthritis sufferer.

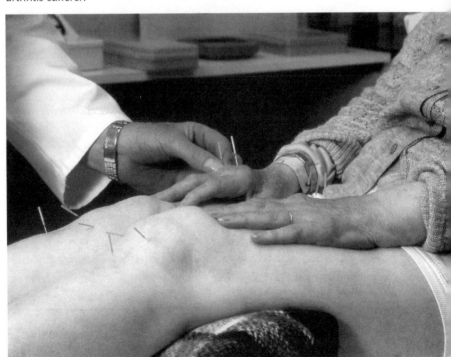

the National Institutes of Health as a treatment for pain, acupuncture is offered in many pain clinics throughout the United States. Moreover, it is one of a few alternative treatments that has licensed practitioners and uses equipment that is regulated by the Food and Drug Administration. As a result, it has become one of the most popular and widely accepted alternative treatments for arthritis. In fact, approximately 15 million arthritis patients have tried acupuncture.

Acupuncture is an ancient form of Chinese medicine that involves the insertion of hair-thin needles into specific points in the body where acupuncturists believe energy channels are blocked. The needles are believed to stimulate the flow of energy through these points, relieving pain. Despite the lack of evidence proving that these energy channels do exist, research has shown that acupuncture significantly reduces the symptoms of arthritis. In fact, it has been shown to be so effective that in one study, 25 percent of arthritis patients scheduled for joint replacement surgery no longer needed the operation as a result of acupuncture treatments. According to rheumatologist Dr. Stuart S. Kassan, "Acupuncture can be very helpful for pain. Rheumatologists see a lot of patients with problems we can't do anything about, especially chronic pain. This is where acupuncture makes its greatest impact with patients who have failed conventional treatment."[30]

Chiropractic treatment is another physical treatment used as an alternative therapy for arthritis. Performed by licensed health professionals, chiropractic treatment involves applying mild force to the spine in order to relieve pressure on nearby nerves. Chiropractors believe that this pressure on the nerves causes disease and damage to the body. Although this theory has not been proven, many patients find relief from pain through chiropractic therapy. Chiropractic treatment appears to be most effective in relieving pain in the neck and back. Experts are not sure why this is so. However, chiropractic therapy has become such a popular form of treatment that the National Institutes of Health are currently studying its effects on the body. One patient who claims that chiropractic treatment eases his pain and stiffness talks about his experience: "It relieves pressure and loosens up my joints. After a session with the chiropractor, I'm always in less pain. I always feel better."[31]

A woman receives a massage on her hand and wrist to alleviate her arthritis pain.

Massage is another alternative treatment that involves the rubbing, kneading, and stroking of the body. Massage can be done over the whole body or can be concentrated on one or two areas. Often performed with soothing music playing in the background and aromatic candles burning, massage has been proven to relax the muscles, easing tension and increasing relaxation and the production of endorphins. In many cases, massage has been found to offer enough pain relief to allow patients to begin exercising. According to an arthritis patient who is helped by massage, "It completely relaxes me. The whole atmosphere is quiet and comforting. There's classical music playing softly. Lavender-scented candles fill the air. The therapist gently rubs my sore body with warm oil. It's like riding on a cloud. By the time she finishes, all my aches and pains melt away."[32]

Treatments That Use the Mind

Meditation is another popular alternative treatment that many experts and arthritis patients endorse. In meditation, patients use concentration techniques such as silently repeating a word or a chant to clear the mind in order to relax the body and lessen pain. Many experts believe that meditation promotes healing by calming the immune system, thus lessening inflammation and improving joint function.

Two women participate in tai chi, an ancient treatment that can improve the mobility of an arthritis patient.

A number of studies have found that meditation can lower stress, improve sleep, and lessen chronic pain. The connection between meditation and pain relief is so strong that many hospitals, universities, and health organizations offer courses in meditation. A survey by the Arthritis Foundation of doctors who treat arthritis found that 59 percent recommend meditation as an alternative treatment. "I meditate for twenty minutes a day," an arthritis patient explains. "It keeps my mind still and drains away my pain. My mind and my body relax. I feel so peaceful and so much better afterwards. The best part is that meditation can't hurt me, the way drugs did, and it's free. There is no drug in the world that works like meditating."[33]

Tai chi is another ancient treatment that uses physical and mental techniques to ease sore joints and relieve pain. Often referred to as "meditation in action," tai chi, like acupuncture, was developed in ancient China as a way to improve mental and physical health by increasing the flow of energy throughout the body. Still popular in China today, tai chi is used by Chinese doctors as a preventive therapy and treatment for almost every disease including arthritis. Tai chi is a form of exercise that promotes relaxation by using the whole body in a series of controlled movements that improve balance and strengthen the joints while regulating breathing and inner thoughts. Exactly how tai chi affects the body is unclear, but experts agree that tai chi does improve arthritis patients' mobility and relieves pain.

Scientific studies reviewed by the National Institutes of Health have shown that tai chi lowers blood pressure, improves balance and flexibility, and results in an improvement in the quality of life for people with chronic diseases. In fact, regular use of tai chi reduces falls among people who have problems with balance, including many arthritis patients. Interest in tai chi is so strong that the National Institute of Aging is currently studying its effectiveness. Moreover, it is such a popular alternative treatment among arthritis sufferers throughout the world that the Arthritis Foundation of Australia has designed a tai chi program specifically for arthritis patients. The creator of this program, Dr. Paul Lam, a physician and arthritis patient himself, has been practicing tai chi for thirty years to keep arthritis in his neck, back, and hands under control. According to Dr. Lam, "Tai chi takes the joints gently through a range of motion, while the emphasis on breathing and inner stillness relieves stress and anxiety. There is no doubt that tai chi, done properly, can be beneficial for people with arthritis."[34]

Dietary Supplements

Dietary supplements such as vitamins, minerals, and chemicals found in the body, and also a wide variety of herbs, have been a common way to treat arthritis for many years. Herbs, in particular, have been a traditional treatment for arthritis for centuries. In fact, from medieval times until the twentieth century, when other medicines were developed, doctors prescribed herbal remedies in tea or pill form as a primary treatment for arthritis. Herbal remedies use the leaves, stems, and roots of certain plants that are known to have healing properties. Many conventional medicines prescribed today are made by mixing herbal extracts with chemicals.

Since herbal remedies use only natural plant parts, users feel that they are gentler than traditional medicine. Today, herbs still remain a very popular alternative treatment for many patients for whom conventional drug treatment has failed. In fact, Americans spend $2.5 million a year on herbal medicine, and research from the American College of Rheumatology has shown that specific herbs such as angelica, alfalfa, boswellia, and cat's claw reduce inflammation. Other herbs like burdock, bromelain, ginger, and capsaicin relieve pain. A combination of such herbs provides relief from multiple symptoms of arthritis.

Perhaps the most popular dietary supplement used to treat arthritis is a combination of the sugar compound glucosamine and the protein chondroitin sulfate, which are both found naturally in the body. Though it is considered a new treatment, glucosamine and chondroitin sulfate have actually been used for many years by veterinarians to treat arthritis in animals. Unlike other alternative treatments for arthritis, this supplement is believed not only to relieve pain and stiffness but also to slow down the progress of arthritis and possibly help cartilage to heal itself. Experts believe that, in its natural state, glucosamine is involved with cartilage formation and repair, and chondroitin sulfate gives cartilage its elasticity. Scientists theorize that, in supplemental form, these chemicals work to strengthen joints and prevent arthritis.

Though inconclusive, the results of recent studies concerning the compound are promising. One recent study found that glucosamine and chondroitin sulfate was more effective in relieving arthritis pain than some nonsteroidal anti-inflammatory drugs. Another study found that it slowed cartilage damage in some patients. Research acknowledges that there is even the possibility that it may stimulate the rebuilding and growth of cartilage.

Although the glucosamine and chondroitin sulfate compound has not been irrefutably proven to be effective, many patients believe it has helped them. Dr. Dean Goodman recalls the successful treatment of one of his patients:

> Before consulting me he had steroid injections, physical therapy, and oral medication, which later resulted in severe stomach complications. They only served as temporary remedies. Having become desperate, he considered knee surgery. He began a series of collagen injections and took an oral supplement containing glucosamine and chondroitin sulfate. Within several weeks—and for the first time in more than two years—his discomfort and swelling was subdued, his mobility increased, and he was able to sleep through the night again. Nearly a year later, it appears that his relief will most likely be permanent.[35]

Homeopathy

Still another dietary form of alternative treatment that many arthritis patients turn to is homeopathy. Developed in the eighteenth century, homeopathy involves treating disease with minute doses of substances derived from plants, minerals, and animals that are believed to cause the disease. Unlike conventional drug treatment that tries to relieve symptoms, homeopathic treatment actually tries to worsen symptoms in an effort to stimulate the body into healing itself. This is done by analyzing the root of the patient's symptoms and the patient's personality, and then designing an individual remedy to treat the patient from more than two thousand homeopathic remedies that have been diluted countless times.

Despite the absence of evidence that homeopathic treatment is effective, more than 200 million Americans seek homeopathic treatment each year. Among them are many arthritis sufferers who believe that the individualized nature of homeopathic treatment, which treats the whole person rather than merely the symptoms, has helped them to feel better. A patient who attributes homeopathic treatment for helping her physically and emotionally explains, "I swear by arnica [a homeopathic medication] for pain and anxiety. I'm usually a nervous person, but with arnica my nerves aren't as jittery. Feeling calmer helps keep my pain levels down. By helping me emotionally, arnica helps me physically. Besides making me sick, standard medicine just treated my pain, not my emotional state."[36]

Unconventional Treatments

As a result of the large number of people who find standard drug treatment ineffective, a thriving industry offering alternative treatments for arthritis has developed. Many of these treatments appear to offer patients relief, but the effectiveness and safety of others are more controversial. Among the most controversial treatments are those that claim to be based on "secret" formulas that offer miracle cures for arthritis, when no cure currently exists. These controversial methods often use "mysterious" or questionable ingredients.

Injections with the venom from bee stings, and with dimenthyl sulfoxide, a powerful chemical used in paint thinner, fall into this category. Although experts are unsure why, studies in Asia have shown that bee venom reduces arthritis pain. Chemicals in dimenthyl sulfoxide are also believed to act as a pain reliever. Less hazardous are unconventional treatments such as color therapy, where certain colors are projected onto sore joints in the belief that different wavelengths of light have healing properties, and the wearing of magnetic shoes and copper bracelets. Wearers believe that a magnet's magnetic pull blocks pain, and traces of copper, which enter the bloodstream through the wearer's pores, soothe inflammation.

Although in some cases these treatments can be successful, many experts believe that in general the relief they give patients is due to the unpredictability of arthritis or the placebo effect, in which the patient's strong belief that a treatment will work results in success, rather than because of the efficiency of the treatment.

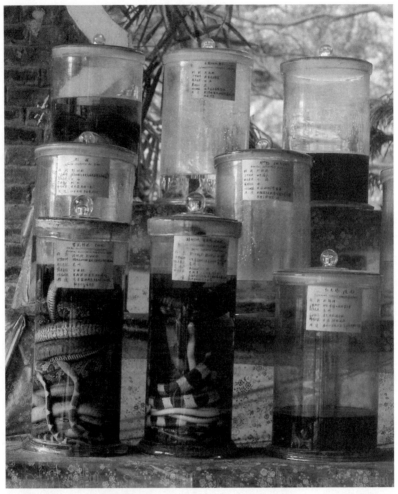

Some alternative, homeopathic arthritis treatments include making medicinal wines derived from snakes.

What Doctors Think

Many doctors are suspicious of these treatments because of their unproven effectiveness. They can also cause other problems as well. For example, megadoses of vitamins commonly used as an alternative treatment by many arthritis patients can accumulate to toxic levels, posing a grave danger. For this reason, 50 percent of doctors surveyed by the Arthritis Foundation advise patients against using this treatment.

Despite these problems, many doctors do believe that when certain alternative treatments are combined with traditional treatments, in a method known as complementary treatment, they can be effective. As a result, doctors often supply patients with the names of reputable alternative practitioners and, in many cases, help patients develop a complementary treatment plan. In such a plan, patients are encouraged to combine alternative treatments such as medita-

Meditation is touted as another alternative treatment for arthritis pain.

tion or acupuncture to relieve pain with conventional treatments such as DMARDs to control joint damage and exercise to strengthen muscles. According to rheumatologist Dr. Justus Fletcher, "I believe in a comprehensive approach, using conventional and alternative therapies and the power of positive thinking. The key is adding to—not subtracting from—conventional medicine. I suggest many alternative therapies, using a little of this and a little of that, designed for the individual patient."[37] Among the alternative therapies that Dr. Fletcher has successfully combined with traditional treatment are acupuncture, meditation, tai chi, and glucosamine and chondroitin.

According to a survey conducted by *Arthritis Today* magazine, 85 percent of the doctors surveyed believed that some alternative therapies are effective, and 49 percent of these doctors recommend them. With this in mind, a growing number of doctors are providing their patients with care that integrates traditional and alternative treatments. One such doctor, Dr. Beth Reiss, explains why: "There's just too much evidence that some of these things do help people. And too many people are using these therapies. We need to be able to guide them."[38]

How Safe Are Alternative Treatments?

Just as conventional treatments can pose serious health risks, so can alternative treatments. One of the greatest risks occurs when people replace conventional treatment with alternative treatment. Although alternative treatment may temporarily improve these patients' symptoms, it will not stop joint destruction. Often, patients take this course of action without consulting their doctor who can assess the effectiveness of the conventional medicine. For this reason, 73 percent of arthritis doctors surveyed by the Arthritis Foundation were concerned about the possible permanent damage and disability that can occur when patients substitute alternative treatments for conventional ones.

The lack of regulations for many alternative products and the lack of mandatory licensing for many alternative practitioners can also present health risks. Even seemingly harmless alternative treatments such as massage can be damaging, since rubbing the body increases circulation, which can worsen inflammation.

In fact, even treatments performed by certified practitioners that have been proven effective can pose health risks. Chiropractic treatment is one such treatment that can sometimes be damaging to arthritis patients, since applying pressure to already damaged joints can often make them worse. "I went to a chiropractor because my hip was bothering me," an arthritis patient explains. "The treatment hurt. She pulled my legs and my neck to try to make me even and used some sort of vibrator on my hip. When I got home I felt terrible. I could barely walk. I was in so much pain that I had to stay home from work the next day. It took me days before I could walk normally."[39]

Risks may also arise from the use of herbs and other dietary supplements. Complicating treatment with these substances is the lack of set dosages. Unlike the monitoring of conventional medicine, in which government agencies supervise the level of active ingredients, the levels of active ingredients in herbs and other dietary supplements are not monitored, even when the ingredients may be as powerful as those found in prescription drugs. Unaware of this, many patients assume that because they are natural, these products are safe. However, this is not always true. Herbs and supplements may be too strong, causing a bad reaction. In fact, there have been cases in which the strength of herbal products has been found to be three times the amount stated on the label. High doses of certain herbs can cause vomiting, heart problems, strokes, and even paralysis. Moreover, patients are just as likely to have an allergic reaction to herbs and supplements as they are to drugs.

Further complicating matters is that, in the absence of government regulations, unknown ingredients may be used. According to studies by the National Center for Environmental Health, some herbal products do not contain the ingredients listed on their labels, while others contain a mix of herbs and drugs. When these drugs and herbs interact, the result can often cause problems for arthritis patients whose weakened immune systems are often quite vulnerable.

Even one of the most widely studied and recommended alternative treatments, glucosamine and chondroitin sulfate, can cause damaging side effects. The presence of sulfates and animal tissue and cartilage extracted from crabs, shrimps, lobsters, or sharks in this supplement can cause severe allergic reactions in some patients.

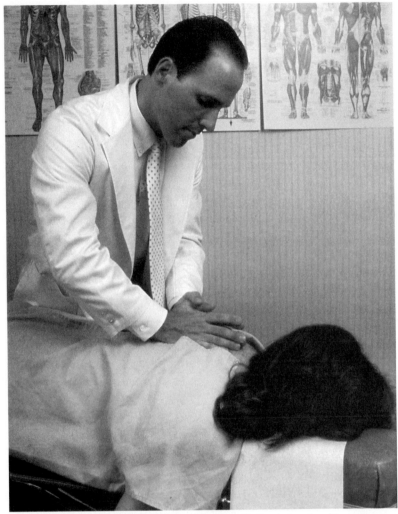

A woman receives treatment for her arthritis with the help of a chiropractor.

It can also raise blood sugar levels, which can lead to diabetes; act as a blood thinner, which makes blood clotting difficult; and cause cholesterol levels to rise, which contributes to heart disease. "I took glucosamine and chondroitin for about six months. When I went for my yearly physical, my cholesterol level had skyrocketed," a patient reports. "My wife read that glucosamine and chondroitin can raise your cholesterol. Sure enough, when I stopped taking it, my cholesterol dropped back down to normal."[40]

Limited testing on even the most promising alternative treatments has resulted in inadequate scientific data on their effectiveness, leading to confusion among both patients and experts about which treatments are helpful and which are not. In addition, insufficient studies to determine whether alternative products are safe have led many patients to experience unexpected and dangerous side effects. Unlike with conventional treatments, which must pass strict testing before being approved by the Federal Drug Administration, regulations on alternative products are weak. However, these possible health risks have not stopped millions of desperate arthritis patients, who have found conventional drug treatments ineffective, from turning to alternative treatments. Dr. Earl J. Brewer explains: "When you have tried just about everything else and you are still in pain and unable to function normally, you may, understandably, be looking for other possibilities."[41]

Chapter 4

Living with Arthritis

ARTHRITIS AFFECTS PEOPLE'S lives in many different ways. It presents both shared and specific challenges to adults and children. Depending on the type and severity of arthritis patients have, chronic pain, joint destruction and deformities, fatigue, and loss of mobility frequently make daily activities a challenge. No matter what their age, many arthritis sufferers find it difficult to perform simple routines, causing numerous changes in their lives. For example, people with damage to their wrists, hands, or fingers often may not be able to perform tasks that involve using their hands. Trouble grasping and squeezing, combined with limited strength, make everyday activities like turning the pages of a book, writing, operating a computer, wrapping a present, and using a knife and fork difficult for these people. Housework is another challenge for sore and stiff patients who cannot bend or reach. In fact, getting out of bed, standing for more than a few minutes, and walking from room to room can be an unfeasible chore for patients with seriously damaged knees, hips, and feet. A patient whose arthritis changed his life discusses its impact on his daily activities:

> I have arthritis in both hips. My range of outward motion in each hip is quite limited—I find that I can no longer swing my leg over my bicycle's top bar. I cannot sit well in a chair or on a sofa, and car seats aren't any better. I walk kind of side to side. Sometimes I cannot sleep well. Often, but not always, I cannot easily rise out of a chair and step forward. I cannot bend down easily and pick something off the floor.

Simple tasks, like turning pages, become a challenge for arthritis sufferers.

Despite these problems, by using the right approach this patient leads an active, productive, and happy life. He continues, "I must exercise every day. My wife and I folk dance. Although my range of motion is affected, the exercise, music and friends help physical problems disappear. I have found that the exercises I do, the supplements I take, plus the spiritual practice I have are helping me to maintain the life I enjoy."[42]

Coping with Chronic Pain

Even with the right approach, perhaps the greatest challenge to daily living is coping with chronic pain, a problem that affects arthritis patients of all ages. According to Dr. Barry Fox, "Pain has a way of enveloping your mind, hijacking your brain, and making it difficult to concentrate on work, families, hobbies, or anything else. You desperately want to be fully involved in life, but the pain distracts, worries, irritates, and depresses you to the point where you can't think of anything else. The things you used to do with ease become difficult or even impossible to accomplish."[43]

This type of long-lasting pain disturbs sufferers when they're awake and asleep. Experts estimate that sleep problems caused by chronic pain occur in 90 percent of all arthritis patients. Arthritis sufferers report being unable to turn over, raise their arms over their heads, bend their knees, or pull the blanket into place, and once asleep, pain often awakens them during the night. Consequently, many arthritis patients never experience REM, the part of sleep that allows the body to rejuvenate and repair itself. As a result, they often wake up feeling weak and drowsy, which makes performing normal activities difficult. Many patients report that simple activities such as a trip to the grocery store use up much of their energy. Often, patients must change or cancel their regular activities in order to deal with their exhaustion. To meet this challenge, arthritis experts and patients agree that one of the most effective tools that people with arthritis can use is pacing themselves to conserve energy. This involves balancing difficult activities with rest periods. Therefore, naps are frequently part of arthritis patients' days.

Sometimes, due to pain and fatigue, arthritis patients have trouble coping. At these times, many arthritis sufferers depend on help from others. Assistance from family and friends allows many patients to handle challenging situations. As an arthritic teenager explains, "Sometimes I can't even eat because either my wrists hurt too much to hold the fork, or my elbows won't bend far enough to reach my mouth. Some days I can't brush my teeth, wash my hair or get dressed. My parents have to do everything for me."[44] In addition to family and friends, home health care workers who come to patients' homes and help them dress, prepare meals, shop, and do housework often provide extra assistance.

Pain and Fatigue Lead to Depression

Even with the help of others, the combination of pain and fatigue frequently causes stress, which can weaken the immune system and result in flare-ups. Making matters worse, emotional reactions to stress can result in the development of depression. Research acknowledges that many arthritis patients of all ages develop depression, which can affect their ability to concentrate, make them lose interest in daily activities, increase fatigue and pain, and cause fear and anxiety. Scientists believe that there may be a link between severe arthritis and depression, which afflicts more than 20 percent of arthritis patients. An arthritis patient who suffered from depression talks about his experience: "I found myself listless, with no energy and no interest in anything. I had almost a physical sense of being tied or weighted down as though every movement was a struggle."[45]

Anxiety and fear caused by depression often result in both adult and juvenile arthritis patients giving up social activities. According to arthritis expert Dr. Harris H. McIlwain, "Many people with arthritis worry about leaving the safety of their home. One woman missed her son's law school graduation because of fear of falling in the airport. A gentleman did not attend his granddaughter's wedding [for similar reasons]."[46] This inability to make plans causes both patients and their loved ones to become frustrated. As a result, these patients may receive fewer and fewer social invitations, leading them to feel lonely and isolated. To guard against depression, experts advise arthritis patients to do whatever it takes to reduce pain and limit stress. With this advice in mind, it becomes clear that patients' approaches toward their pain affect the quality of their lives considerably.

Limited Mobility Challenges Adults and Children

Loss of mobility also creates daily challenges for people of all ages with arthritis. In a survey by the Arthritis Foundation, 80 percent of the arthritis sufferers polled said that loss of mobility made every aspect of their daily lives more difficult. Patients reported difficulty caring for themselves and their families. In addition, 81 percent of the patients surveyed reported feeling that they are no longer in control of their own lives. Still others reported worrying about losing their independence in the future. One arthritis patient says, "I don't think in terms of pain so much as I think in terms of restricted motion and limited freedom. My independence is more important to me than anything else."[47]

Being unable to work or attend school and being dependent on others are real and frightening possibilities for these patients. They report facing such threats to their independence as losing their abil-

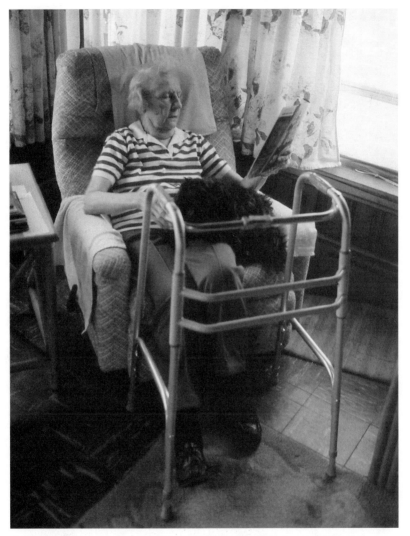

Arthritis sufferers who have lost mobility often depend upon walkers for assistance.

ity to drive, being unable to stand for extended periods of time, and being unable to walk without a cane, crutch, walker, or wheelchair.

Despite such problems, most people with arthritis adjust their circumstances in order to maintain their independence. A patient who had trouble dressing himself talks about how he handled this challenge and maintained his independence:

Dressing can be a great pain. Putting on socks and shoes in the conventional manner became very difficult for me (socks, in fact, became impossible), as did putting on underwear and pants. But you don't have to dress yourself in the conventional manner; you can change both your environment and the way you interact with it.

If you have to wear shoes that tie, you don't have to bend down to tie them while your foot rests on the floor. I put one foot on top of the other. That much additional elevation turned an impossible task into a simple one for me. [48]

Protecting the Joints

To meet the challenges that arthritis poses, and to maintain their independence, many children and adults with arthritis use special devices that are designed to protect their joints. These devices prevent patients from putting unnecessary stress on already weakened joints, thus minimizing further joint damage. Splints are one type of joint savings device. Made of molded plastic or metal and strapped to the joint with an elastic bandage, splints provide protection, support, and rest for the joint. Often, even simple activities like shaking hands can be challenging and damaging for arthritis sufferers. Wearing a splint can rectify this problem. According to one patient, "When I am going to be somewhere that I expect a lot of handshaking I wear my wrist splints. Most people will just gently take the fingertips when you reach out with a splint. Not the prettiest option, but it works!" [49]

Similarly, specially molded shoes protect people whose feet have been deformed by arthritis. These shoes are custom made from castings of the patient's feet. Although not stylish, they provide the wearer with greater stability and support, thus keeping the patient more mobile.

Other devices designed to alleviate problems resulting from damage to specific joints allow patients to be more active and self-reliant. For example, rubber grips on scissors, pencils, cookware, and doorknobs; special key and doorknob turners; zipper pulls; and stretch shoelaces assist patients whose fingers are too weak for gripping and who might otherwise be unable to perform these everyday tasks. Similarly, voice-activated phones and telephone headsets help make life easier for patients who can't bend their neck or hold a phone. Reaching devices also help patients pull on socks or grab items they would otherwise be unable to bend or reach for. In addition, canes, crutches, power scooters, wheelchairs, and power seat lifts help patients with damage to their legs, feet, or hips get in and

A caliper splint keeps the ankle in a fixed position allowing an arthritis patient to walk without moving the ankle joint.

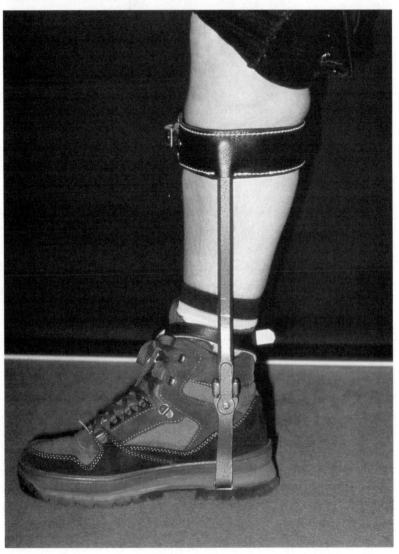

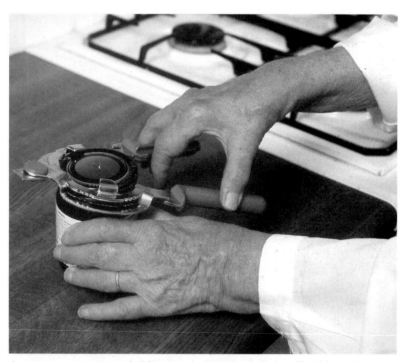

A woman uses a manual aid to open a jar. Many devices like this assist arthritis sufferers with their everyday activities.

out of chairs and remain mobile. According to one arthritis sufferer, "I love my collapsible cane. If I am going any place where I might have to walk a lot, I carry this cane in a large purse or tote bag. When, and if I need it, it is there ready for me to use."[50]

By changing unhealthy movement habits and maintaining correct posture, patients protect their joints from undue stress and injuries. Many patients turn to an occupational therapist who trains them in the principles of joint protection. Such principles include using strong, large joints instead of small, weak ones. For example, patients with arthritis of the hands or fingers learn to use their healthy shoulders to carry things. This makes daily living at home, at work, and at school easier. An occupational therapist also instructs patients on ways to adapt their surroundings to accommodate their disabilities. Activities such as using a box or stand to prop up a book while reading, or sitting on a bar stool while washing dishes, help make everyday tasks easier, allowing arthritis patients to be more independent.

Maintaining Balance

Arthritis experts and patients agree that the key to maintaining an independent lifestyle is balance. Both young and old patients who accept their limitations and adapt their lives accordingly are more likely to take more pleasure from life. "At first," a patient recalls, "I tried to do too much."

> The arthritis overwhelmed me. There were many things that became more and more difficult to do, especially since I've always been extremely active. Then I realized I couldn't be Superwoman, I had to pace myself. I learned to slow down and make a few changes. I take a walk instead of jogging. I have a lady clean my house. I nap when I'm tired. I try to simplify whatever I can. I use

An arthritis-support group gathers to perform sit-down exercises and to share information and encouragement.

little tools like a rolling stool that I sit on while I garden because it's painful to bend, and long-handled tongs for picking up around the house. I stretch and move around at work so my joints don't stiffen up. I wear flat shoes instead of the high heels I used to adore. I realize I can't do everything I used to do, but there are lots of things I can do instead.[51]

Another important tool that helps arthritis sufferers of all ages maintain balance in their lives is support groups. Participating in support groups makes patients feel like they are taking an active part in managing their lives, which results in decreased pain and fatigue. These groups give members a chance to share their feelings in addition to providing information, encouragement, and a sense of belonging. By sharing their common experiences, support group members often find solutions to problems that non–arthritis sufferers do not understand. "Our meetings," one patient explains, "consist of much talking, getting things off our chests, some guest speakers, and most of all being able to relate to others who understand what we are going through. Communicating with others who understand is truly a godsend."[52]

Medical Monitoring

Frequent visits to the doctor for both preventive care and special monitoring are another aspect of all arthritis patients' lives. Experts estimate that 20 percent of arthritis patients are afflicted with drug-related health problems such as stomach ulcers and liver and kidney problems. As a result, they must be checked often to prevent problems from arising. Furthermore, statistics show that people with inflammatory forms of arthritis are more prone to developing infections and cancer than other people are. Scientists theorize that this may be due to a combination of the medication these patients take and their abnormal immune systems.

By having frequent physical exams and blood tests that can detect cancer and other diseases, arthritis patients can protect themselves from drug-related diseases and lengthen their lives. They are also required to take annual flu and pneumonia shots. In addition, just like the general population, arthritis patients are advised to eat nutritiously, drink little or no alcohol, and not smoke. However, this advice is even more important for arthritis patients than for other people because this lifestyle serves to strengthen their weakened immune systems. Experts agree that when arthritis patients have their medical condition frequently monitored and make sensible lifestyle choices, they are less likely to develop illnesses that can shorten their lives.

Children with Arthritis

Medical monitoring is especially important for children with arthritis. Forty percent of juvenile arthritis sufferers develop iritis, a painless inflammation of the eye, that when left untreated, can cause permanent blindness. Experts believe that the presence of special proteins called antinuclear antibodies, which are found only in the blood of many juvenile arthritis sufferers, triggers the development of this disease, but they are unsure why this is so.

Children with arthritis may also face other medical problems such as problems with their growth. Because juvenile arthritis patients' joints are damaged and deformed, growth in the affected joints is often slowed down. As a result, many juvenile arthritis sufferers are quite small for their age. This affects not only their appearance but also how others deal with them. A young girl explains how this affects her: "I am really small in comparison to other grade six students. What I have the most trouble with is people talking to me as if I am much younger. I hate when they baby talk to me and of course, there is the clothes issue. Thank God my mom can sew."[53]

The problem of deformed joints caused by juvenile arthritis can also cause one leg or arm to be longer than the other. The resulting changes in these patients' appearances and the development of a limp are often especially challenging to children and teenagers who want to fit in with their peers but are faced with being physically different. In fact, some juvenile patients report being teased about the way they move. This causes many juvenile arthritis sufferers to become self-conscious about their appearance, and anxious about how others will react to them. Frequently, they will try to hide their differences. A young woman with arthritis remembers her experience: "Starting high school and being around a lot of new kids was rough. My old friends were used to me. But when I started high school, I

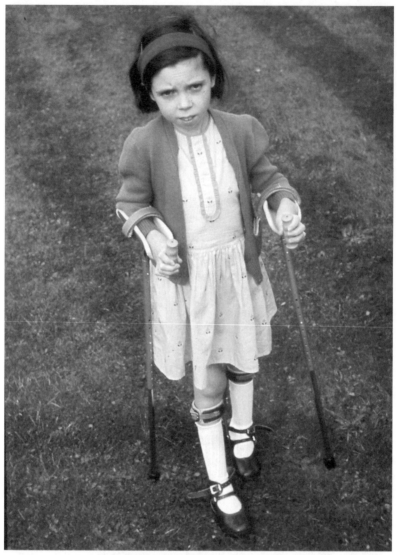

Pictured is a girl with rheumatoid arthritis. Children with arthritis can suffer from growth irregularities and joint deformities.

was in a big school with all these new people. I wanted to fit in. I was very self-conscious about the way I moved. I didn't want anyone to see me limp."[54]

Such physical changes, combined with persistent pain and limited mobility, often cause changes in young patients' lifestyles. During flare-ups, juvenile arthritis sufferers may be absent from school for prolonged periods of time. As a result, many opt to be home-schooled. Those who attend school may have difficulty sitting in hard chairs, raising their hands, taking notes, carrying heavy books, and moving from class to class. Often these students must leave class early to get to the next class on time, and may have special permission to use the elevator. A teenager with arthritis describes her typical school day: "I go to school every day, usually hardly able to walk. I hobble through the halls very slowly and painfully, and I am often tardy for my classes. I have tremendous trouble sitting down from a standing position, and especially in standing up from a sitting position. Sometimes my wrists hurt so much that I cannot write. Yet still, each day, I must somehow manage to do all these things and then be able to make it through the day."[55]

Other problems arise during the school day for patients who must take medication that causes drowsiness and memory loss. Because of this, they may be less alert and able to concentrate during class. One patient tells how this affected her: "My memory and attention are not that great. My medicine fogs up my brain. When I was taking a dose during school, my grades went right into the Dumpster. I really messed up on my final exams. I couldn't remember what we learned a week ago, so forget about the beginning of the semester. Having arthritis doesn't make school any easier."[56]

Besides academic challenges, students with arthritis are often unable to fully participate in physical education classes. Many must sit on the sidelines and watch while their friends play. Those who can participate frequently have to give up participation in sports that are too damaging to their joints, such as track, gymnastics, football, soccer, basketball, and baseball. A baseball player and juvenile arthritis sufferer explains why he was forced to stop playing baseball: "Even my hands hurt when I held the bat. And when I take a swing, my shoulders kill."[57]

Like all arthritis sufferers, juvenile arthritis patients who are forced to give up a favorite activity, often feel discouraged about not being able to live their lives as they did before contracting arthritis. However, unlike adults, the youngest arthritis sufferers, with their limited experience, may not be fully able to understand that arthritis cannot be cured. Instead, they often believe that if they do whatever their parents and doctor ask them to, their arthritis will eventually disappear and their lives will return to normal. Unfortunately, this is not so. An arthritis patient recalls her experience as a young girl:

> I was diagnosed with arthritis when I was a little girl. Being so young, I had no idea what arthritis was. I knew that I was in pain, and I knew that it was serious. It wasn't like getting hurt playing basketball because instead of going away, the pain spread all over my body. I couldn't do any of the things I liked to do. I didn't even want to, because of the pain. At one point I could barely dress my Barbies. I kept hoping that the doctor would give me a shot and I'd be cured. I mean, that's what happened in the past when I got sick. But it didn't happen. There were doctor's visits, and bad-tasting medicine, and therapy sessions, and I never was cured. That was probably the hardest part, I didn't understand what was happening to me. [58]

One way that many children and young adults with arthritis learn more about what is happening to them and how to deal with it is by spending their summers attending special camps for juvenile arthritis patients that are sponsored by the Arthritis Foundation. These camps help juvenile patients learn ways to meet the challenges they face every day. They also give them a chance to participate in physical activities that accommodate their limitations and have fun with other children and young adults like themselves. One such camper explains how this camp helps her: "I love spending time with other children and young adults who have juvenile rheumatoid arthritis because it gives us all a feeling of normalcy that kids with these diseases struggle to find in our peer groups." [59]

A Delicate Balance

With the support of the new friends they make in camp and their family, most juvenile arthritis sufferers go on to lead active and happy lives. According to Dr. Earl J. Brewer and Kathy Cochran Angel, "With coordinated care and continuous support, children with arthritis have the best chance for living a well-adjusted life and entering the mainstream of adulthood with hope and confidence." [60]

A woman with arthritic hands peels an apple. Active lives can be lead if arthritis patients balance their limitations and abilities.

Similarly, when patients of all ages follow a related course, balancing their limitations with their abilities and focusing on whatever it takes to improve their situation, the results are quite positive. As one patient explains,

> I've never known not having arthritis. In some ways I think I'm lucky because I don't have the same sense of loss that other people have because I never really knew anything else. I had a very forward-looking father that knew computers were where it was at. And he would always tell me, "You are not going to be able to do real physical things, you are going to have to use your mind." After college I got a job with Hewlett-Packard, which was my dream. I grew up being told that I would never be able to have a career, drive or live on my own. It's been my goal in life to prove everybody wrong.[61]

Like this patient, most people with arthritis are not defeated by the challenges they face. By making necessary adaptations and maintaining positive attitudes their lives are active, productive, and happy.

Chapter 5

What the Future Holds

D OCTORS HAVE RESEARCHED the many forms of arthritis and discovered how to manage the pain that comes with the disease. What remains unsolved is why some people get arthritis while others do not and what causes the disease.

Groups such as the National Institutes of Health, the National Institute of Arthritis and Musculoskeletal and Skin Diseases, and the Arthritis Foundation have dedicated all their efforts to research. Working with a number of pharmaceutical companies, these groups have joined together to provide about $21 million per year for arthritis studies. Much of this research centers on trying to solve the mystery of who gets arthritis and why. Scientists believe that focusing on the roles that genetics and the immune system play in the development of the disease will garner the greatest results. They believe that the knowledge they gain will lead to the discovery of new and better treatment strategies, which will decrease both the development of arthritis and the damage it causes, thus improving arthritis patients' quality of life.

No Cure in Sight

Focusing on who gets arthritis and why, rather than seeking a specific cure for arthritis, distinguishes arthritis research from research into more lethal diseases such as AIDS or cancer, where the need to find a cure is more critical. Although, as is true with all diseases, scientists would like to find a cure for arthritis, researchers acknowledge that at this time such a discovery is unlikely. In fact, researchers are not certain that a cure will ever be found. The problem lies in the fact that arthritis is not one simple disease but, rather, a group of more than one hundred related diseases, each extremely complex and each with different distinguishing features. Consequently, even if scientists did find a cure, it would probably not work on every type of arthritis.

Further complicating the discovery of a cure is that even if scientists did manage to find a cure that worked for most currently existing forms of arthritis, new forms of arthritis are still being

Two hands with early and advanced stages of arthritis compared to a normal hand (right).

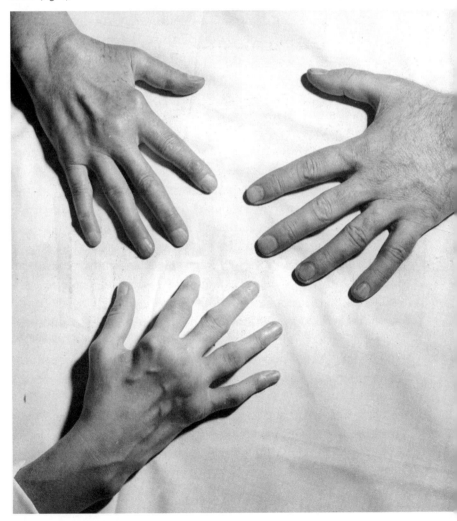

discovered. Experts doubt that such a cure would also be effective on newly discovered forms of the disease. For these reasons, scientists feel that they can best serve arthritis patients by determining what, if any, genetic and immune factors predispose certain people to getting arthritis. This, they believe, will help them to develop new techniques to prevent or lessen the effects of the disease.

Genetic Factors

Researchers are beginning to find new data on the role that genes play in the development of arthritis. Genes are tiny cells found in every living thing that determine individual traits such as hair color, eye color, and artistic talent. Because genes are passed down from parents to children, scientists have been analyzing population data, seeking a relationship between the genetic transmission of arthritis among family members. Their studies indicate that multiple relatives throughout many generations are often victims of arthritis. Studies that examined twins with arthritis yielded similar results. These studies found a high incidence of identical twins, who share identical genes, who both had the disease.

In an attempt to uncover a particular gene that causes arthritis, researchers have been studying family members afflicted with the disease. Working with the Arthritis Foundation and the National Institutes of Health, researchers throughout the United States have been collecting data from more than one thousand families who have two or more siblings with arthritis in order to pinpoint common genetic factors. Their findings suggest that all of the family members in the study with arthritis have a faulty gene that interferes with the production of collagen, a protein that strengthens cartilage. All the unaffected family members in the study lack this gene. Scientists theorize that the presence of this particular gene weakens cartilage, making people with it more susceptible to arthritis.

Other research has found that multiple family members with arthritis often have a slight defect in the way their bones and joints fit together. This defect, commonly known as double-jointedness, allows their joints to bend farther at different angles. It also may result in their cartilage wearing away faster than usual, putting them at greater risk of developing arthritis. Because this trait is frequently

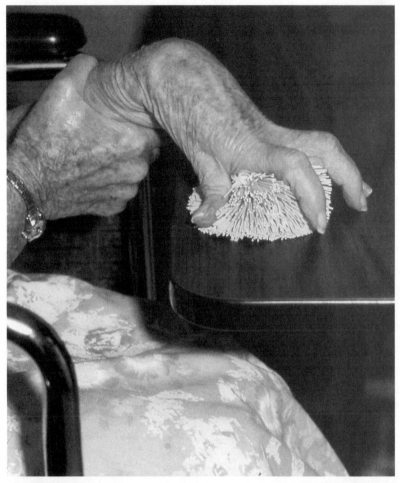

An elderly woman with an arthritic hand participates in a physical therapy session.

found among family members, researchers believe it is caused by another, as yet unidentified, specific gene.

There is mounting evidence that other genes play distinct roles in the development of arthritis as well. One such gene labeled HLA-DR4 has been found repeatedly in people with rheumatoid arthritis. Another gene, HLA-B27, has been found in people with ankylosing spondylitis. These genes have not been found in people without these forms of arthritis. Scientists believe that people who possess these particular genes are more likely to develop these diseases.

Moreover, scientists theorize that there may be a different, specific gene involved in the development of each of the more than one hundred types of arthritis.

Immune Factors

While many scientists are studying the role genetics plays in who gets arthritis and why, others are attempting to solve this riddle by examining the immune system. A number of studies are investigating how the immune system is controlled, how the different parts of the immune system relate to each other, and how individual cells in the immune system get signals. Since the immune system is so com-

A T cell stimulates a B cell in an experiment to see if the B cell will attack a joint.

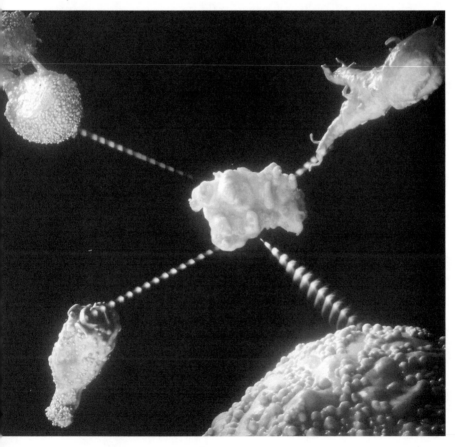

plex and has so many different components, researchers are focusing these studies on examining specific parts of the immune system and the role that each part plays in autoimmune disease in hopes of preventing or stopping the autoimmune response. Scientist Dr. David Pisetsky, who is involved in this research, explains: "We're trying to find different molecules involved in the process and better ways to block this assault." [62]

With this in mind, scientists at the University of Alberta, Canada, are investigating a group of white blood cells known as T cells. T cells act like signalmen and warn the rest of the immune system when the body is threatened by germs. Their warning signal is the starting point in a long chain reaction of at least fourteen steps that sets the immune system into attack mode. Scientists theorize that many people with inflammatory arthritis have abnormal T cells. These abnormal T cells are believed to start a similar chain reaction that results in an autoimmune attack on the joints. By starting with the abnormal T cells and following the chain step by step, scientists expect to be able to pinpoint at exactly what step the attack on the joints is signaled. Once this is accomplished, a form of treatment that will halt the reaction at the signal point will be searched for. Such a treatment could stop the attack on the joints before it begins. According to one of the researchers in this study, Dr. Nancy Dower, "There will be a lot of interest in finding ways to affect this step. Once you know the step, you can figure out ways to turn off the process." [63]

Farther along this chain, other white blood cells, named B cells, are released. Essential to an autoimmune reaction, B cells are believed to be the white blood cells that actually attack the joint lining. Researchers are currently studying B cells in the hopes of learning enough about these attackers to develop a drug that will target and destroy them before they damage the joint lining.

Two different powerful antibodies or proteins, called interleukin and tumor necrosis factor, are next in the chain. Scientists hypothesize that these proteins are responsible for inflaming and destroying cartilage. Researchers in California and Seattle are studying interleukin and tumor necrosis factor in the hopes of developing drugs that could stop their destructiveness. Known as protein blockers,

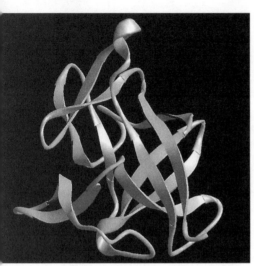

The interleukin protein is believed to be responsible for destroying joint cartilage.

such drugs would act like roadblocks, stopping the damaging proteins from reaching the cartilage. One such protein blocker is currently being tested on human volunteers in tests known as clinical trials. The results are promising.

How Genetics Affects the Immune System

Many scientists are convinced that specific problems in the immune system may be the result of mutant genes. A study in Great Britain has found a mutant gene that causes the immune system in mice to work incorrectly. Researchers theorize that this gene is responsible for the immune system being overactive, as it is in inflammatory arthritis, and also for it being underactive, as it is in diseases like AIDS. If researchers can learn enough about this gene, they predict that they will be able to develop drugs that would work with this gene to either stimulate or subdue the immune system, depending on the disease. According to the director of this study, Dr. Robert Jackson, "We have validated that this gene is a virtual off/on switch for the immune system and, depending on the disease, there are times when we need to turn the system off and times when we need to turn it on. We now have a new pathway to use in the discovery and development of drugs for unmet medical needs."[64]

Canadian scientists have discovered a different gene that may determine the severity of rheumatoid arthritis. Like the gene discovered in Great Britain, this gene, known as the IFN gamma gene, is instrumental in the operation of the immune system. Certain abnormalities in the gene appear to increase the level of joint inflammation in rheumatoid arthritis patients. Scientists speculate that patients with the mutant IFN gamma gene are more likely to be stricken with severe rheumatoid arthritis than patients without this gene. Researcher Dr. Abbas Khani-Hanjani reports that "It is the most powerful indicator currently recognized for predicting the severity of arthritis." [65]

Experts anticipate that tests for this genetic abnormality will be developed in the future to help doctors predict just how severe a patient's arthritis will become. This will help doctors to formulate an individual treatment plan for patients early in the disease, which would include aggressive treatment if the IFN gamma gene is found. According to Arthritis Society researcher Dr. Dianne Lacaille, "It offers the possibility of identifying early which patients are likely to get severe disease and selecting appropriate treatment before joint damage has occurred." [66]

This test would also allow patients who test negative for the gene to be treated with milder, less risky, and less expensive drugs than might otherwise be used. Rheumatologist Dr. Edward Keystone explains: "If I knew that a patient has a good prognosis, I'm not going to use a toxic medication. I'm not going to use some of the new biologics that cost between ten thousand and seventeen thousand dollars a year." [67]

The Value of Genetic and Immune System Research

Without a doubt, studies on genetics and the immune system are crucial factors in determining who gets arthritis and why. These studies hold great promise in helping arthritis patients now and in the future. Knowing that, because of genetic factors, people who have family members with arthritis are more likely to contract the disease themselves can help these people make lifestyle adjustments that protect their joints and, hopefully, prevent or delay the onset of arthritis. In the future, once specific genes involved in causing arthritis have been identified, the use of genetic tests to identify people who possess these mutant genes will be a remarkable tool for predicting and diagnosing arthritis. Even more exciting is the prospect of preventing the development of arthritis through the use of new therapies that could repair gene errors before arthritis flares up. Although this type of gene therapy is not yet fully developed, its potential for preventing the onset of arthritis is tremendous. According to arthritis researcher Dr. Roland Moskowitz, "Eventually we may be able to repair the gene error. Of course, such technology is years away, but we may be able to prevent certain forms of arthritis decades before the disease develops."[68]

By learning more about how the immune system works and identifying specific abnormalities in it, scientists hope to develop more efficient treatment methods that will target and inhibit specific abnormalities without suppressing the rest of the immune system, as many current treatments do. This type of treatment should protect patients from many health problems caused by their entire immune system being suppressed. Medical writer Christine Gorman, reporting from a meeting of the American College of Rheumatology, states,

Pictured is finger-joint swelling due to synovitis, a symptom of rheumatoid arthritis.

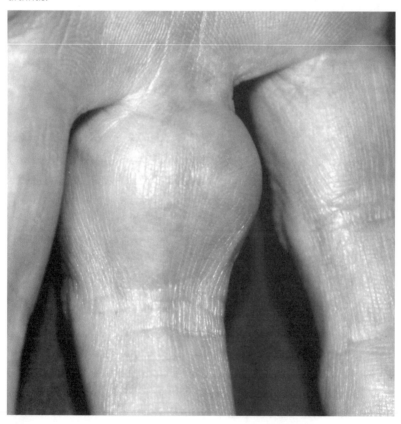

For the past fifteen years, doctors have tried to treat the underlying disorder with the pharmaceutical equivalent of a sledgehammer, using drugs and steroids to beat down the body's hyperactive defense force. What researchers now realize is that to treat the joint disease they don't have to clobber the whole immune system, just certain portions of it. Nor do they have to destroy their targets. They can merely stun them momentarily.[69]

Tissue Engineering

Using the knowledge that they are amassing about genetics and the immune system, scientists are experimenting with tissue engineering, a complex new technology that involves altering faulty cells by removing them and replacing them with synthetically created cells.

Researchers are exploring three types of tissue engineering. In the first type, enzyme engineering, cells that produce chemicals that destroy inflamed cartilage and joints are replaced with genetically altered cells. The new cells would be specifically modified to block the production of these dangerous chemicals, thus preventing further damage to the joint from occurring. For example, cells that produce the damaging interleukin and tumor necrosis factor would be replaced with new cells that stop the production of these harmful proteins.

Similarly, in cartilage cell replacement, another type of tissue engineering, damaged cartilage cells are removed and replaced with new, healthy cloned cells. These new cells would be injected directly into the patients' joints, where they would multiply and weave themselves together, patching damaged cartilage. In current studies, replacement cartilage cells have only been able to repair about one inch of damaged cartilage. However, researchers predict that, in the future, cartilage cell replacement will be used to treat larger areas, making it an effective treatment for lessening the symptoms of arthritis.

The final form of tissue engineering, stem cell transplantation, involves transferring special healthy cells, derived from adult tissue and from embryos, into damaged joints and cartilage. Researchers believe that these cells, known as stem cells, are capable of changing into and repairing almost any cell in the human body. With this in mind, scientists theorize that if stem cells were transplanted into damaged joints and cartilage, they would transform into new, healthy joints and cartilage. If successful, such a procedure would replace and repair damaged cartilage and joints, making joint replacement surgery obsolete.

Scientists theorize that stem cells could also be used to repair the immune systems of people with inflammatory arthritis. In a clinical trial conducted at Northwestern University, doctors tested this theory by introducing new stem cells into the immune systems of subjects with severe lupus. The doctors presumed that the stem cells would replace mutant T and B cells in the subjects' damaged immune systems. The results were quite promising. All of the subjects went into complete remission for at least two years. During this time, their immune systems functioned normally. The doctors concluded that stem cells transplanted into the immune systems of inflammatory arthritis patients do not make the same mistakes as the mutant cells they replace, resulting in long-term relief. Although treatment with this procedure is still experimental, experts are optimistic that it will be a valuable tool in the future.

The Role of Food and Nutrition

While trying to piece together the puzzle of who gets arthritis and why, scientists have found evidence that certain dietary practices, combined with genetic and immune factors, may predispose some people to contract arthritis. Ongoing research has linked both nutritional deficiencies and overindulgence in other nutrients to the development of arthritis or the worsening of arthritic symptoms. Moreover, alcohol abuse and smoking have also been connected to the development of the disease.

A number of studies have indicated that a deficiency of omega 3 fatty acid, a nutrient found in fish, increases inflammation. Conversely, studies have shown that diets rich in this nutrient appear to stop inflammation and improve pain and stiffness. In fact, research indicates that people who eat at least two servings of fish rich in omega 3 fatty acid each week are 43 percent less likely to develop arthritis than people who are deficient in this nutrient. Interestingly, ancient physicians often used cod liver oil, a fish oil that is rich in omega 3 fatty acid, as an effective treatment for arthritis. Many people with arthritis are already taking omega 3 fatty acid supplements in the hope of combating the symptoms of the disease. However, because large doses of this supplement can often cause negative side effects, scientists are currently trying to develop a form that will be easier to tolerate. Experts theorize that such a pill

Diets that include plenty of fish may prevent joint inflammation and alleviate arthritis pain.

would be a highly effective and safe treatment for inflammation, pain, and stiffness.

Other studies that examine deficiencies of boron, a nutrient found in fruits, vegetables, beans, and nuts, point to a link between the development of arthritis and deficiencies of this nutrient. Once again, researchers theorize that diets rich in boron help relieve pain and inflammation and inhibit the development of arthritis. Although scientists are unclear exactly what boron's role is in combating arthritis, researchers hypothesize that this nutrient is important in strengthening and building bones.

Although studies have shown that a diet rich in omega 3 fatty acid is good for arthritis, other studies have indicated that another fatty acid, omega 6, which is found in many fast foods and processed foods, produces a substance that actually triggers inflammation and increases the pain of arthritis.

In addition, other studies have been examining the role that purines, nutrients found in alcoholic beverages and in organ meats such as liver and kidneys, play in arthritis. Results indicate that overindulgence in these foods and in alcohol can cause the body to overproduce uric acid, a chemical that is often linked to the development of gout.

Still other studies have been searching for a connection between smoking and arthritis. One study done at the University of Alabama found that subjects who smoked were twice as likely to develop arthritis as nonsmokers. Another study that examined the relationship between arthritis patients who smoked and the severity of arthritis they were afflicted with found that smoking was associated with increased inflammation and pain. Why this is so has not been determined. Although these studies are not conclusive, there is mounting evidence that smoking weakens bones and joints.

Altering Diet

Although none of the information on the role nutrition plays in the development of arthritis conclusively proves that a deficiency or excess of any one nutrient can cause arthritis, scientists hypothesize that dietary factors can trigger the disease, especially in people who

Alcohol use and smoking can increase a person's chances of developing arthritis.

are genetically predisposed to it. Rheumatologist Dr. Beth Karlson explains: "It may be that you have to have the right genes that put you at high risk, and it could then be twenty-five different low-risk environmental factors that give the susceptible person the disease."[70] Scientists include nutritional factors, alcohol use, and smoking among these environmental factors.

Hope for the Future

It is clear that the progress scientists have made in understanding who gets arthritis and why has already improved available treatments and lowered people's risk of contracting the disease. As research continues and pieces of the arthritis puzzle are continually found, even more effective treatments and prevention methods will be developed, and someday, scientists hope, a way of preventing arthritis will be discovered.

Notes

Introduction: A Disease That Affects Individuals and Society
1. Tara, interview with the author, Dallas, TX, February 10, 2001.
2. Tara, interview with the author.

Chapter 1: What Is Arthritis?
3. Quoted in Derrick Brewerton, *All About Arthritis: Past, Present, Future.* Cambridge, MA: Harvard University Press, 1992, p. 121.
4. Barry Fox and Nadine Taylor, *Arthritis for Dummies.* Foster City, CA: IDG Books, 2000, p. 13.
5. Quoted in CreakyJoints.com, "Whose Fault Is It?" www.creaky joints.com/creakyjoints/write/write0001.shtml.
6. Earl J. Brewer Jr. and Kathy Cochran Angel, *The Arthritis Sourcebook.* Los Angeles: Lowell House, 1999, p. 149.
7. Quoted in CreakyJoints.com, "Whose Fault Is It?"
8. Quoted in Roderick Jamer, "Wings of Angels, Feet of Clay," *Arthritis News Magazine,* vol. 11, No. 4, 1993. www.arthritis.ca.
9. Joel Rutstein, "Arthritis Central Case #3," Arthritis Central. http://arthritiscentral.com.
10. Fox and Taylor, *Arthritis for Dummies,* p. 35.
11. Meg, interview with the author, Dallas, TX, February 15, 2001.
12. John, interview with the author, Dallas, TX, February 24, 2001.
13. Arthritis Foundation, "Managing Activities." www.arthritis.org/ AFStore/StartRead.asp.
14. Quoted in Brewer and Angel, *The Arthritis Sourcebook,* p. xii.
15. Meg, interview with the author.

Chapter 2: Diagnosis and Treatment
16. Cleo, interview with the author, February 16, 2001.
17. Arthritis Research Campaign, "About Arthritis," www.arc.org.uk/ common/about_arth_f.htm.

18. Quoted in Brewer and Angel, *The Arthritis Sourcebook*, p. xi.
19. Fox and Taylor, *Arthritis for Dummies*, p. 300.
20. Cleo, interview with the author.
21. Marilyn, telephone interview with the author, March 10, 2001.
22. Meg, interview with the author.
23. Quoted in Brewer and Angel, *The Arthritis Sourcebook*, p. 113.
24. Quoted in Shelly Morrison, "Exercise Success Stories," *Arthritis To-day*, January 1999. www.arthritis.org/ReadArthritisToday/1999_archives/1990_01_02exercise.asp.
25. Quoted in Harris H. McIlwain and Debra Fulghum Bruce, *Stop Osteoarthritis Now*. New York: Fireside, 1996, p. 37.
26. John, interview with the author.
27. Quoted in Ronald J. Allen, Victoria Anne Brander, and S. David Stulberg, *Arthritis of the Hip and Knee*. Atlanta: Peachtree Publishers, 1998, p. 199.
28. Quoted in Arthritis Insight, "Tips and Hints." http://arthritis insight.com/living/ tips1.html.

Chapter 3: Alternative Treatment
29. Barb, interview with the author, Dallas, TX, February 22, 2001.
30. Quoted in Judith Horstman, "Acupuncture," *Arthritis Today*, May 2000. www.arthritis.org/ReadArthritisToday/2000_archives/2000_05_06_acupuncture.asp.
31. John, interview with the author.
32. Cleo, interview with the author.
33. Barb, interview with the author.
34. Quoted in Judith Horstman, "Tai Chi," *Arthritis Today*, July 2000. www.arthritis.org/ReadArthritisToday/2000_archives/2000_07_08_taichi.asp.
35. Dean Goodman, "New Nutrient Compound Can Rebuild Damaged Cartilage," *Journal of Longevity*, vol. 6, no. 3, 2000, pp. 23–24.
36. Marilyn, interview with the author.
37. Quoted in Arthritis Foundation, "More than Medicine," *Arthritis Today*, March/April 2001. www.arthritis.org/resources/arthri..._archives/2001_03_04_MoreThanMedicine.asp.
38. Quoted in Judith Horstman, "Why Doctors Aren't Asking and You Aren't Telling," *Arthritis Today*, November/December 1999.

www.arthritis.org/ReadArthritisToday/1999_archives/1999_11
_12alternatives.asp.

39. Barb, interview with the author.
40. John, interview with the author.
41. Brewer and Angel, *The Arthritis Sourcebook*, p. 146.

Chapter 4: Living with Arthritis

42. Quoted in Arthritis Foundation, *The Arthritis Foundation's Guide to Good Living with Osteoarthritis.* Atlanta: Arthritis Foundation, 2000, p. 109.
43. Fox and Taylor, *Arthritis for Dummies*, p. 125.
44. Quoted in JRA World, "Member Stories." http://jraworld.arthritis insight.com/community/stories/therese.html.
45. Quoted in Allen, Brander, and Stulberg, *Arthritis of the Hip and Knee*, p. 50.
46. McIlwain and Bruce, *Stop Osteoarthritis Now*, p. 222.
47. Quoted in Morrison, "Exercise Success Stories."
48. Quoted in Allen, Brander, and Stulberg, *Arthritis of the Hip and Knee*, p. 35.
49. Quoted in Arthritis Insight, "Advice for Better Living Archives." www.arthritisinsight.com/living/advice/archive.html.
50 Quoted in Arthritis Insight, "Tips and Hints." www.arthritis insight.com/living/tips.html.
51. Julia, interview with the author, Dallas, TX, March 4, 2001.
52. Quoted in Arthritis Foundation, *The Arthritis Foundation's Guide to Good Living with Osteoarthritis*, p. 25.
53. Quoted in JRA World, "Social Factors." www.arthritisinsight.com/ cgi-bin/wsmbb/wsmbb.cgi?RT+RXDZPIOWPQ/OJVZZXZBUC+ 1852+0+JRAWorld+5582722.
54. Meg, interview with the author.
55. Quoted in JRA World, "Member Stories." http://jrworld.arthritis insight.com/community/stories/therese.html.
56. Meg, interview with the author.
57. Quoted in *Current Health 1*, "Oh My Aching Joints," December 1998, p. 29.
58. Tara, interview with the author.
59. Quoted in JRA World, "Member Stories." http://jraworld.arthritis

insight.com/community/stories/mindy.html.

60. Brewer and Angel, *The Arthritis Sourcebook*, p. 73.

61. Quoted in Michele Taylor, "Working for a Living," Arthritis Foundation. www.arthritis.org/ReadArthritisToday1999_archives/1999_05_06roundtable.asp.

Chapter 5: What the Future Holds

62. Quoted in Sandra W. Key and Daniel J. DeNoon, "4.3 Million NIH Grant Received for Study," *Disease Weekly Plus*, November 3, 1997, p. 24.

63. Quoted in Andy Ogle, "Missing Step in Body's Battle Against Disease Discovered," *Edmonton Journal*. www.edmontonjournal.com/city/stories/001015/4691107.html.

64. Quoted in About.com, "Autoimmune System Activating Gene Discovered." http://pharmacology.about.com/health/pharmacology/library/98news/bln0929c.htm.

65. Quoted in Wired News, "Genes May Aid Arthritis Treatment," www.wired.com/news/print/0%2C1294%2C38428%2C00.html.

66. Quoted in Wired News, "Genes May Aid Arthritis Treatment."

67. Quoted in Wired News, "Genes May Aid Arthritis Treatment."

68. Quoted in Joseph Wallace, "Can Arthritis Be Prevented?" *Arthritis Today*, July/August 1990, p. 46.

69. Christine Gorman, "Relief for Swollen Joints," *Time Magazine Online*, October 28, 1996. www.time.com/time/magazine/archive/1996/dom/961028/medicine.relief_for_swol5.html.

70. Quoted in Hakon Heimer, "Autoimmune Diseases—Risk Factors," *Environmental Health Perspectives*, October 1999, p. 507.

Glossary

aerobic exercise: Exercise that builds stamina and strengthens the heart.

alternative practitioner: A person who offers unconventional medical treatments.

ankylosing spondylitis: A form of arthritis that affects the spine.

antibody: A special protein found in the immune system that attacks foreign invaders.

antinuclear antibodies: Proteins found in the blood of many juvenile arthritis patients.

assistive devices: Tools that help handicapped people make day-to-day living easier.

autoimmune disease: A disease in which the body attacks itself.

autoimmune response: A reaction of the white blood cells that causes them to attack healthy cells in the body.

B cell: A type of white blood cell that is believed to attack the joint lining during an autoimmune response.

boron: A nutrient found in fruits and vegetables that is believed to relieve inflammation.

carpal tunnel syndrome: A form of arthritis that affects the hand and fingers.

cartilage: A connective tissue that covers and cushions the ends of bones.

cartilage cell replacement: A type of tissue engineering that entails removing damaged cartilage cells and replacing them with healthy cells.

clinical trials: Medically supervised research of new medication using human volunteers as subjects.

collagen: The main protein found in bones and cartilage.

conventional treatment: Medical treatments studied in American medical schools.

dietary supplements: Vitamins, minerals, and other nutrients that are taken in addition to food.

disease-modifying antirheumatic drugs (DMARDs): Medication that treats arthritis by modifying the way the immune system works.

double-jointedness: The ability of certain joints to bend more than what is normal.

endorphin: A natural chemical produced by the brain that creates a feeling of well-being.

enzyme engineering: A technology that involves replacing cells that produce chemicals that destroy inflamed cartilage with genetically altered cells.

flare-ups: Periods when arthritis symptoms are at their worst.

flexibility-building exercise: Exercises that help to make the body limber.

foreign substance: Something that is not part of and doesn't belong in the body.

gastrointestinal bleeding: Internal bleeding in the stomach and intestines.

glucosamine and chondroitin sulfate: A popular dietary substance that is used to treat arthritis.

gout: A form of arthritis that affects the big toe.

IFN gamma gene: A gene that is believed to be an indicator of severe rheumatoid arthritis.

immunosuppressants: Drugs that keep the immune system from malfunctioning.

inflammation: Reaction to infection and injury that results in swelling, redness, and heat.

interleukin: A protein that causes inflammation and destruction of cartilage.

juvenile arthritis: A form of arthritis that affects children and teenagers.

lupus: A form of arthritis that can lead to inflammation of the heart, lungs, and kidney.

megadoses: More than the generally acceptable dosage of a dietary supplement.

mobility: The ability to move around.

musculoskeletal: Having to do with muscles and bones.

nonsteroidal anti-inflammatory drugs (NSAIDs): Drugs that do not contain steroids but relieve inflammation.

occupational therapist: A licensed professional who helps handicapped people cope with the problems they face in daily living.

omega 3 fatty acid: A nutrient found in fish that is believed to relieve inflammation.

omega 6 fatty acid: A nutrient found in processed foods that is believed to worsen inflammation.

orthopedic surgeon: A doctor who specializes in operating on bones.

osteoarthritis: A form of arthritis caused by the breakdown of cartilage.

placebo: An ineffective medication, such as a sugar pill, often used in research studies as a control.

purine: A nutrient found in organ meat that is believed to worsen the symptoms of gout.

remission: Periods when arthritis patients have no symptoms and feel normal.

repetitive movements: Movements that are performed over and over.

rheumatoid arthritis: A form of inflammatory arthritis that occurs when the immune system attacks itself.

rheumatoid factor: An antibody found in the blood of many rheumatoid arthritis sufferers.

rheumatologist: A doctor who specializes in the treatment of arthritis.

rheumatology: The study of arthritic diseases.

stem cell transplantation: A type of tissue engineering that involves removing healthy cells and inserting them into damaged parts of the body.

steroid drugs: Man-made medication that works like human steroids in fighting inflammation.

steroids: Inflammation-fighting hormones found in the human body.

stomach ulcers: Holes in the walls of the stomach.

strength training: Exercises that build muscle and strength.

synovial fluid: A fluid found within joints that keeps the bones from grinding against each other, and helps the joints to move easily.

T cells: White blood cells that are believed to signal other cells to attack.

tendons: Tough fibers found at the ends of muscles that attach to bones.

tissue engineering: A type of technology that involves altering faulty cells by removing them and replacing them with synthetically created cells.

tumor necrosis factor: A protein that causes inflammation and destruction of cartilage.

uric acid: A chemical produced by the body that is involved in the development of gout.

weight-bearing joints: Large joints such as the hips and knees that support the body.

Organizations to Contact

American Juvenile Arthritis Organization
1330 West Peachtree St.
Atlanta, GA 30309
(404) 965-7524
Internet: www.arthritis.org/answers/children_young_adults.asp

This organization offers support and information about juvenile arthritis.

Arthritis Foundation
1314 Spring St. N.W.
Atlanta, GA 30309
(800) 283-7800
Internet: www.arthritis.org

The Arthritis Foundation provides support, information, and funds for arthritis research. It offers a large variety of free informational pamphlets; a magazine, *Arthritis Today*; videotapes; self-help courses; clubs and support groups; water-exercise programs; and lists of doctors who specialize in treating arthritis. There are many local chapters.

National Center for Complementary and Alternative Medicine
Clearinghouse
P.O. Box 8218
Silver Springs, MD 20907-8218
(888) 644-6226
Internet: http://altmed.od.nih.gov/hccam

This organization conducts research on the effectiveness of alternative treatments and provides information on a wide variety of alternative treatments.

National Institute of Arthritis, Musculosketal and Skin Diseases Information Clearinghouse
1 AMS Circle
Bethesda, MD 20892-3675
(877) 226-4267
Internet: www.nih.gov/niams

This institute funds research on arthritis and provides information.

For Further Reading

Books

Virginia Tortorica Aldape, *Nicole's Story: A Book About a Girl with Juvenile Rheumatoid Arthritis*. Minneapolis: Lerner Publications, 1996. This book, geared to young readers, discusses how juvenile arthritis affects one young girl's life.

Madelyn Klein Anderson, *Arthritis*. New York: Franklin Watts, 1989. A simplified overview of what arthritis is and how it is diagnosed and treated.

Arthritis Foundation, *Arthritis 101: Questions You Have, Answers You Need*. Marietta, GA: Longstreet Press, 1997. Questions and answers about every aspect of arthritis.

Judith Horstman, *The Arthritis Foundation's Guide to Alternative Therapies*. Marietta, GA: Longstreet Press, 1999. This book discusses alternative treatments for arthritis and their effectiveness.

Mary C. Powers, *Arthritis*. New York: Chelsea House, 1992. This young adult book explains what arthritis is, how it is treated, and how it affects patients' lives.

Shelley Peterman Schwarz, *250 Tips for Making Life with Arthritis Easier*. Marietta, GA: Longstreet Press, 1997. This book gives tips on different ways to make living with arthritis easier.

Brian R. Ward, *Bones and Joints*. New York: Franklin Watts, 1991. A simplified explanation of how bones and joints work.

Websites

Anna's JRA Page (www.geocities.com/tlzeigler/AnnasJRA.html). This website is a mother's personal account of her daughter's life with juvenile arthritis. It offers a number of links specific to juvenile arthritis.

Arthritis Central (http://arthritiscentral.com). This website provides information and case studies about arthritis.

Arthritis Foundation (www.arthritis.org). This website offers information on many different types of arthritis, tips on coping with arthritis, free pamphlets, forums, on-line access to *Arthritis Today* magazine, and support for people with arthritis.

Arthritis Insight (www.arthritisinsight.com). This website offers information, advice, and support from people with arthritis. It includes news, discussion groups, and links.

Arthritis Society of Canada. (www.arthritis.ca). This website offers information about all aspects of arthritis and articles about its impact on society. It provides support for people with arthritis in Canada.

CreakyJoints.com (www.creakyjoints.com). This website offers support and humorous articles about living with arthritis.

JRA World (http://jraworld.arthritisinsight.com). This website deals with juvenile arthritis. It provides information about the disease and treatment options, on-line support, chat rooms, message boards, inspirational stories, and jokes.

Works Consulted

Books

Ronald J. Allen, Victoria Anne Brander, and S. David Stulberg, *Arthritis of the Hip and Knee*. Atlanta: Peachtree Publishers, 1998. This book looks at the causes of and treatment options for arthritis of the hips and knees, and focuses on the different aspects of surgery. It follows one patient's experience from the development of arthritis to postsurgery.

Arthritis Foundation, *The Arthritis Foundation's Guide to Good Living with Osteoarthritis*. Atlanta: Arthritis Foundation, 2000. This book gives patients the tools to understand and manage osteoarthritis. It includes many personal accounts of people who are controlling the disease.

———, *Understanding Arthritis*. New York: Charles Scribner, 1984. This book explains what arthritis is, how it is treated, and how to cope with it.

Earl J. Brewer Jr. and Kathy Cochran Angel, *The Arthritis Sourcebook*. Los Angeles: Lowell House, 1999. This book discusses the symptoms, diagnosis, treatment, and challenges of living with arthritis.

Derrick Brewerton, *All About Arthritis: Past, Present, Future*. Cambridge, MA: Harvard University Press, 1992. The history of arthritis research and how scientific knowledge about this disease has developed.

Barry Fox and Nadine Taylor, *Arthritis for Dummies*. Foster City, CA: IDG Books, 2000. This book gives a wealth of information about every aspect of arthritis in an easy-to-read format.

Harris H. McIlwain and Debra Fulghum Bruce, *Stop Osteoarthritis Now*. New York: Fireside, 1996. An examination of osteoarthritis that includes possible treatment options.

Ray Porter, *Medicine: A History of Healing*. New York: Marlowe, 1997. This book looks at ancient and modern methods of treating diseases.

Periodicals
Current Health 1, "Oh My Aching Joints," December 1998.

Dean Goodman, "New Nutrient Compound Can Rebuild Damaged Cartilage," *Journal of Longevity*, vol. 6, no. 3, 2000.

Hakon Heimer, "Autoimmune Diseases—Risk Factors," *Environmental Health Perspectives*. October 1999.

Sandra W. Key and Daniel J. DeNoon, "4.3 Million NIH Grant Received for Study," *Disease Weekly Plus*, November 3, 1997.

Deborah Kotz, "Are Herbal Remedies Safe for Kids?" *Good Housekeeping*, July 2001.

Newsweek, "Arthritis," September 3, 2001.

Prevention, "Earlier Arthritis Treatment Pays Off," September 2000.

Joseph Wallace, "Can Arthritis Be Prevented?" *Arthritis Today*, July/August 1990.

Internet Sources
About.com, "Autoimmune System Activating Gene Discovered." http://pharmacology.about.com/health/pharmacology/library/98news/bln0929c.htm.

Arthritis Foundation, "Managing Activities." www.arthritis.org/AFStore/StartRead.asp.

———, "More than Medicine," *Arthritis Today*, March/April 2001. www.arthritis.org/resources/arthri...archives/2001_03_04_More ThanMedicine.asp.

Arthritis Insight, "Advice for Better Living Archives." www.arthritis insights.com/living/advice/archive.html.

———, "Arthritis Tips and Hints." www.arthritisinsight.com/living/tips1.html.

CreakyJoints.com, "Brain over Body." www.creakyjoints.com/creaky joints/write/write0002a.shtml.

———, "Whose Fault Is It?" www.creakyjoints.com/creakyjoints/write/write0001.shtml.

Christine Gorman, "Relief for Swollen Joints," *Time Magazine Online*, October 28, 1996. www.time.com/time/magazine/archive/1996/dom/961028/medicine.relief_for_swol5.

Judith Horstman, "Acupuncture," *Arthritis Today*, May 2000. www.arthritis.org/ReadArthritisToday/2000_archives/2000_05 _06_acupuncture.asp.

———, "Tai Chi," *Arthritis Today*, July 2000. www.arthritis.org/ ReadArthritisToday/2000_archives/2000_07_08_taichi.asp.

———, "Why Doctors Aren't Asking and You Aren't Telling," *Arthritis Today*, November/December 1999. www.arthritis.org/Read ArthritisToday/1999_archives/1999_11_12alternatives.asp.

Roderick Jamer, "Wings of Angels, Feet of Clay," *Arthritis News Magazine*, vol. 11, no. 4, 1993. www.arthritis.ca.

JRA World, "Member Stories." www.jraworld.arthritisinsight.com.

———, "Social Factors." www.arthritisinsight.com/cgi-bin/wsmbb/ wsmbb.cgi?RT+RXDZPIOWPQ/OJVZZXZBUC+1852+0+JRA World+5582722.

Shelly Morrison, "Exercise Success Stories," *Arthritis Today*, January 1999. www.arthritis.org/ReadArthritisToday/1999_archives/1990_ 01_02exercise.asp.

Andy Ogle, "Missing Step in Body's Battle Against Disease Discovered," *Edmonton Journal*. www.edmontonjournal.com/city/stories/ 001015/4691107.html.

Joel Rutstein, "Arthritis Central Case #3," Arthritis Central. http://arthritiscentral.com.

Michele Taylor, "Working for a Living," Arthritis Foundation. www.arthritis.org/ReadArthritisToday1999_archives/1999_05_0 6roundtable.asp.

Wired News, "Genes May Aid Arthritis Treatment." www.wired. com/news/print/0%2C1294%2C38428%2C00.html.

Websites

Arthritis Research Campaign. (www.arc.org.uk). Offers information about arthritis and current arthritis research.

Index

Picture Credits

Cover photo: © CORBIS
© Patricia Agre/Science Source/Photo Researchers, 73
© Jules T. Allen/CORBIS, 20
Archive Photos, 75
© Lester V. Bergman/CORBIS, 15, 30
Paul Biddle & Tim Malyon/Science Photo Library/Photo Researchers, 45
© Biophoto Associates/Photo Researchers, 11, 19
David M. Campione/Science Photo Library/Photo Researchers, 77
© CORBIS, 80
© Alain Dex/Publiphoto/Photo Researchers, 60
© David E. Edgerton, 53
© Kevin Fleming/CORBIS, 40
© Michael Freeman/CORBIS, 78
Chris Helgren/Reuters, 25
© Walter Hodges/CORBIS, 42
© Ed Kashi/CORBIS, 67
© Liu Liqun/CORBIS, 54
Moredun Animal Health, Ltd./Science Photo Library/Photo Researchers, 17
© John Moss/Photo Researchers, 70
© Larry Muvehill/Photo Researchers, 63
Faye Norman/Science Photo Library/Photo Researchers, 47
© Carolyn Penn/CORBIS, 48
Photo Researchers, 33
Chris Priest/Science Photo Library/Photo Researchers, 27
Princess Margaret Rose Orthopaedic Hospital/Science Photo Library/Photo
    Researchers, 14, 31
Science Photo Library/Photo Researchers, 65, 66, 82
© Paul A. Souders/CORBIS, 22, 85
© Ted Spiegel/CORBIS, 37
© Art Stein/Science Photo Library/Photo Researchers, 57
© James A. Sugar/CORBIS, 38
© Wartenberg/Picture Press/CORBIS, 87

About the Author

Barbara Sheen has been a writer and educator for more than thirty years. Her fiction and nonfiction books, stories, and articles for adults and children have been published in both the United States and Europe. Her work includes bilingual textbooks, children's stories in English and Spanish, and books and stories translated into German. Ms. Sheen holds a master of science degree from Long Island University in New York. She currently lives with her family in Texas, where she enjoys weight training, reading, cooking, and animals. This is her second book in Lucent's Diseases and Disorders series.